THE PHOTOCOPIABLE RESOURCE

Herbert Puchta • Günter Gerngross • Matthew Devitt

Get on Stage!

21 sketches and plays for young learners and teens

HELBLING LANGUAGES

Acknowledgements

We would like to express our boundless appreciation for the continually brilliant work of Mr Pete Durgerian and Headfirst productions; the discerning ear of Mr Al Green at Alsounds; and all the performers, including those from Varndean School, K-Bis school, Brighton Steiner School, Dorothy Stringer School and Shine.

Special thanks for the support of Mr Ed Taljaard, Ms Marcia King, Ms Sami Hayes, Mel Upton, Fliss and particularly Patti Griffiths.

Our thanks to Master Fion Devitt who made things work when we didn't think they would and to Ms Bryony Devitt who made everything that needed making.

And finally, we are indebted to our editorial and production team for their brilliant work: Caroline Petherick, Oonagh Wade, Christina Freudenschuss, Barbara Alt, Francesca Gironi, Elisa Pasqualini, Amanda Hockin, Barbara Prentiss and Gianluca Armeni.

Herbert Puchta, Günter Gerngross and Matt Devitt

Get on Stage!
by Herbert Puchta, Günter Gerngross and Matt Devitt

© HELBLING LANGUAGES 2012
www.helblinglanguages.com

All rights reserved; no part of this publication may be reproduced, stored in a retrieval system, or transmitted in any form or by any means, electronic, mechanical, photocopying, recording, or otherwise, without the prior written permission of the Publishers.
Photocopying of materials from this book for classroom use is permitted.

The publishers would like to thank these sources for their kind permission to reproduce the
following copyright material:
Alamy (CD: Food Icons; Ultimate Food), Dreamstime, iStockphoto, Shutterstock for pictures on p188.

Edited by Oonagh Wade and Caroline Petherick
Copy edited by Caroline Petherick
Designed by Amanda Hockin, BGP Studio, Pixarte
Cover design by Capolinea
Illustrations by Doriano Strologo
Printed by Athesia

Every effort has been made to trace the owners of any copyright material in this book.
If notified, the publisher will be pleased to rectify any errors or omissions.

Contents

		Introduction	4
CHAPTER 1		**Short sketches**	35
	1	The Perfect Son	36
	2	Smart Shoppers	40
	3	A Fast-Food Stall	43
	4	Colin the Poet	48
	5	The Ticket	53
	6	Being Polite	56
	7	Parrot Learns a Lesson	62
	8	Granddad's Birthday	66
	9	The Princess and the Ring	71
	10	At the Doctor's	77
CHAPTER 2		**Medium-length sketches**	87
	11	On Holiday in Rome	88
	12	At the Hairdresser's	96
	13	The Space Restaurant	106
CHAPTER 3		**Medium-length plays based on traditional stories**	115
	14	The Wise Woman	116
	15	The Reward for Kindness	122
	16	Rusty Nail Soup	127
	17	The Children and the Wind	133
	18	The Wise Judge	148
CHAPTER 4		**Teenage dramas**	153
	19	Good Girl	154
	20	The Bully	165
	21	Friendship	172
		Worksheets	183
		Worksheet Key	217
		Quick-reference guide	222
		DVD Contents, Audio CD Tracklist	224

LEGEND   DVD

          Audio CD

Introduction

What is *Get on Stage!* all about?

We have written this book as a response to requests we have frequently heard at language teaching conferences in a variety of countries worldwide. In conversations about what materials colleagues would find useful to support their work, we have often heard requests for ready-made scripts for plays for students to act out. Teachers look for plays that students can perform for each other or in front of a 'real' audience of some sort – be it another class, a group of parents, and/or the school community, at a school fete or maybe at the end of the year. We are using the term 'play' in a generic way here – we mean a range of scripts of different lengths, genres, with different language levels and preparation required.

The plays have been carefully created for young and teenage students (see the introduction to each play). They are easy to stage as they do not require a lot of props – sometimes none at all – and they make it possible for you to involve a large number of students. The introductory notes at the beginning give further suggestions as to how extra students can take part in a play, e.g. by splitting longer roles so that two or more students can play them.

The structure of the book

Get on Stage! has four chapters. Chapter 1 has nine short humorous sketches, each of about five minutes' runtime. There is also one longer sketch (*At the Doctor's*) that has six scenes; however, each of these scenes is a short, self-contained sketch in itself, meaning that you can use the play in a very flexible way. Your students may want to act out just one of the scenes, or several, or all of them.

Chapters 2 and 3 contain plays of medium length (about five to ten minutes, depending on the production). In Chapter 2 you will find three humorous contemporary sketches, and in Chapter 3 five plays based on traditional stories.

The last chapter contains three modern teen dramas; whereas the sketches and plays in Chapters 1–3 can also be used with younger learners, these dramas are specifically for students aged 14–18. For each of the sketches and plays, you are given not only the script but also an introduction. This gives you an overview of the roles and the set and props you may want to use for the performance; then comes a brief description of the style and the synopsis of each play to help you choose the right script for your class. Although the plays are not written to present or practise any particular areas of language, you may find it useful to know roughly what language level your students would need to have acquired to be able to act out the play confidently. So, for easy reference we have given you a description of the expected language level according to the Common European Framework (e.g. Intermediate – B1). Depending on the play, and without any attempt at systematic or comprehensive coverage, we have given some brief listings of examples of, e.g., exponents from certain functional areas, grammar structures, vocabulary sets or high frequency chunks of language.

Introduction

Finally, the introduction to each play gives you stage tips and suggestions for variations. The stage tips provide you with practical suggestions on staging a play or sketch, enabling your students to get the most out of their performance. In the variations sections you can find alternative ideas about what you might do with a sketch or play.

Get on Stage! **comes with a DVD and an Audio CD.**

The DVD

The DVD gives you:

Tips and guidelines for staging and performing a play

The excerpt on the DVD shows Matt Devitt, co-author of *Get on Stage!* and also a theatre director, rehearsing the sketch *Being Polite* (Chapter 1, pp 56–61) with a group of teenage actors. The excerpt shows you different ways of helping your students improve their performance, and focuses on topics that are discussed on pp 18–33 of this introduction: Voice projection; Staging and 'blocking'; Concentration and focus; Building the characters to tell your story; Pace; Set, props, lights, music and sound effects; Changing scenes; and Remembering or learning lines.

We are convinced that the practical tips on the DVD will be of great help in bringing the relevant part of the introduction to life and serve as a good model for your own interventions when rehearsing a play. You may want to watch the excerpt after reading the introduction, then go back and watch it again before you start acting out a play or sketch with your students to remind you of some of the key principles of staging and performing a play. Please note that due to the live nature of the filming, the examples on the DVD do not always follow the order as shown in the introduction.

Video recordings of three sample plays

These plays are acted out on stage by British students. They are:
- *Being Polite* (a short sketch – Chapter 1, pp 56–61),
- *The Space Restaurant* (a medium-length sketch, pp 106–113),
- and *Rusty Nail Soup* (a medium-length play based on a traditional story, pp 127–132)

There is also a short example on the DVD of a 'split scene' technique, demonstrated in a short extract from *Friendship*.

You can show your students the sample plays on these videos for the following purposes:
1) to give them a general idea of how to act out a sketch or a play under normal conditions, i.e. in a classroom or on a school stage without using elaborate props.
2) to give them role models that you can refer to in your own rehearsals. When a student finds it difficult, for example, to project their voice so it can be heard well by the audience, it could be a good idea to play a short extract from one of the videos to the student and ask them to practise by imitating it sentence by sentence.
3) if you are planning to get your students to act out one of those three plays, you can show it to them on the DVD, to demonstrate, for example, how the actors use the

Introduction

stage and interact with one another.

4) alternatively, you could show one or all of these plays in order to give your students some key principles of putting on a play. If you want to do that, we specially recommend *Being Polite*, as the DVD not only shows you a performance of the play by English students, but also gives you examples of how Matt Devitt works with a group of young teenagers and helps them improve their performance. There is another short scene from *Friendship* (a modern teen drama – Chapter 4, pp 172–181); the purpose of this extract is to show you the use of a 'split scene' technique that is used not only in *Friendship* itself, but also in another play in this book, *Good Girl*.

The Audio CD

The Audio CD offers you:

Audio recordings of eleven plays

These plays are spoken in a studio by British children or teenagers. They are:

Track 01	*The Perfect Son*, Chapter 1 pp 36–39
Track 02	*Smart Shoppers*, Chapter 1 pp 40–42
Track 03	*A Fast-Food Stall*, Chapter 1 pp 43–47
Track 04	*Colin the Poet*, Chapter 1 pp 48–52
Track 05	*The Ticket*, Chapter 1 pp 53–55
Track 06	*Parrot Learns a Lesson*, Chapter 1 pp 62–65
Track 07	*Granddad's Birthday*, Chapter 1 pp 66–70
Track 08	*The Princess and the Ring*, Chapter 1 pp 71–76
Track 09	*On Holiday in Rome*, Chapter 2 pp 88–95
Track 10	*The Wise Woman*, Chapter 3 pp 116–121
Track 11	*Friendship*, Chapter 4 pp 172–181

You can use the audio recordings of the sample plays for the following purposes:

1) to develop your students' listening comprehension. For that purpose you might want to use the comprehension tasks that you can find on the worksheets that go with the plays. You can find these on the DVD.

2) the audio recordings can, like the video samples, be used to give students role models that you can refer to in your own rehearsals.

3) if you are planning to get your students to act out one of those plays, you can use the audio recording to help develop their pronunciation and intonation.

4) if you are planning to get your students to act out *Friendship*, you will see in the script (pp 174–181) that we recommend the use of some extracts from pop songs in order to enrich the performance. You may want to encourage your students to select the music that they think is appropriate for the play (see some ideas and also suggestions for songs in the script). Alternatively, you can use some of the short original soundtracks on the CD (tracks 12–16).

Introduction

Photocopiable worksheets

In the appendix of the book you can find a wide range of worksheets. Thumbnails in the introductions to the plays give you a quick overview of the tasks, and remind you of the existence of the worksheets.

- For each of the short plays, there is one photocopiable worksheet containing three activities. These are:
  - an activity that helps students with the comprehension of the play. This can be reading or listening (the latter is possible for all those plays where there is an audio or video recording), and
  - activities for working on the language; for example, vocabulary/chunks of language and/or grammar structures from the script.
- For most of the medium and longer plays there are two pages of photocopiable worksheets giving your students practice in reading and/or listening comprehension, vocabulary, useful phrases, grammar and creative writing.

Why get young learners and teens to act out plays?

In discussions with colleagues, we have frequently heard about the motivational power of plays. We have heard beautiful stories of how parents of children proudly watch a play where their son or daughter appears on stage, and as a result develop more positive attitudes towards their child's school, their child's foreign language learning – and often their teacher as well! We have also heard that otherwise rather inactive teens can suddenly show remarkable amounts of energy when creating props, masks, or costumes, and they can be prepared to rehearse for long hours in order to get the language right. They are happy to listen time and time again to audio recordings of a play so that they can improve their own intonation and pronunciation, and they show remarkable social skills in working together on its preparation. Colleagues who get their students to act out plays have also told us that when they meet their students – sometimes years after they have left school – they often still have fond memories of the day of a special performance.

There is also increasing evidence from cognitive research that supports the use of plays. Learning a foreign language successfully is about taking ownership of it. Our students are learning English as a *foreign language*, but we want to do everything we can to reduce the emotional distance between them and that language. Ownership is about reducing the 'foreignness' of the language to be learnt, about bringing it closer to our students' hearts, getting them to enjoy the new language as a means of expressing themselves, playing with it, and identifying its sounds and intonation patterns. Such processes of identification, imitation and creative play are part and parcel of how children acquire their mother tongue … surely no mother in the whole wide world would ever go into her child's bedroom in the morning and announce, with a big smile, 'Get up my darling – today we're doing the Present Perfect Progressive!' When we

Introduction

are young, we imitate sounds, we play with words, and we act out roles – activities that help children to rehearse important social behaviour, understand how humans act and interact with one another, gain insights into their own behaviour and develop their personality.

Children naturally engage in highly sophisticated 'let's pretend' games, often getting completely absorbed in acting out all kinds of roles that are familiar to them (their mum or dad, a shopkeeper, a policeman), or that they dream up in their imagination. Acting out such roles helps the children to develop their language competences, and their imagination and creativity.

When children become teenagers they go through the challenging phase of adolescence. Now they may appear to be far less prepared to take part in spontaneous role-play activities than they were as young children. However, adolescence is a time of inner fantasy and play. It is at this time of their lives that students need to develop their sense of self – their identity – and identification with role models is part of that process. In their imagination, teens often 'become' the heroes and heroines they admire, and imitate the way they dress, talk, think and act. These heroes and heroines are often the stars of the glitz and glamour of the movie or pop industries, successful sports players or other public figures. Cool teen behaviour in fact is often about imitating others, and a way of pretending that life is anything but difficult during a time when they are often (despite their cool appearance) rather insecure.

We have quite often noticed that adolescents are more than happy to engage in role-play activities. You as a teacher can support this by making sure the atmosphere in the teen classroom is a supportive one, as ridiculing each other is unfortunately a common teen phenomenon. It is worth pointing out to students that you will give them enough time to study their lines and rehearse their performance, as it is important for teens to feel 'safe' in their roles.

The importance of good stories

What are the elements that make a story appropriate for young learners or teenagers? Kieran Egan stresses that by offering the right stories to children a teacher can contribute greatly to the development of their 'cognitive tools'. Stories can support these processes best if they offer strong emotional contrasts, e.g. good vs bad, happy vs sad, foolish vs serious, greedy vs cunning etc. The child needs such stories to be able to develop their own value system and in order to learn what is appropriate and acceptable behaviour and what isn't. As Kieran Egan points out: 'The story form is a cultural universal; everyone everywhere enjoys stories. The story, then, is not just some casual entertainment; it reflects a basic and powerful form in which we make sense of the world and experience' (*Teaching as Story Telling*, University of Chicago Press,

Introduction

1998). Teachers frequently notice that although children learn fast they tend to forget even faster. Offering stories – or, in this case, plays – that are relevant to your students means that students are more likely to remember them, and consequently will also remember the language in a story or play more easily.

As Earl Stevick stresses, most of the sensory information reaching the brain is quickly forgotten. The 'deeper' a sentence is rooted in a student's brain/mind system, the higher the chances that the student will be able to use the language stored later in life. (Earl W. Stevick, *Memory, Meaning & Method*, Second Edition, Heinle & Heinle Publishers, Boston 1996 p. 196)

When students listen to, read or watch a good story, they can become totally absorbed in it, and in their imagination they often become part of the story themselves. When they're acting out a story in the form of a play, the process of identification can become even stronger; they can get so fully engaged in the play that they forget about everything else.

Teenagers go through a phase of changes that is often characterised by a growing interest in the real world. Adolescence is usually a time of emotional turmoil as well. According to insights explained in the educational theories of Kieran Egan, teens – as cool as they may seem on the surface – often feel, deep down, threatened by the world. One reason for their insecurity is the fact that they have no answers to questions they ask themselves. Those questions are of an existentially threatening nature, basically because teens cannot find any answers to them: *Will I be successful in life? Will I be able to find a good job and earn good money one day? When will my parents die? When will I die? What happens when I do? Who will miss me when I die?* etc. Although the world of teens is fundamentally a contact culture, they hardly ever share their real fears with others, and this often leads to a feeling of loneliness and the assumption that they are the only ones in the world suffering from their problems. To them, the only way out of this situation seems to lie in trying *not* to be an individual – not an easy task given that the particular phase in their lives is also about developing their sense of self, their identity – and so they engage in copying each other: wearing the same brands of T-shirts and trainers, adoring the same kind of heroes and heroines, and finding the same kind of things either 'awesome' or 'gross' (current UK teen expressions for 'good' and 'bad'). Such behaviour, together with their choice of heroes, often seem to suggest superficiality to the adult observer. But it's anything but! When teens choose their idols, they do so because they feel intuitively connected with what they perceive as the best human qualities through their heroes, whereas for adults every single one of those stars may well be representative of a tinsel world. Why the difference? Teens project onto their heroes the qualities they believe are needed in order to successfully master the challenges of a threatening world, and whereas it may be true that some of those heroes are pretty scandalous and superficial people themselves, the qualities teens see in them are important human values: love, courage, creativity, tolerance, endurance, engagement, solidarity, passion, and

Introduction

especially the ability to have got themselves into a place where they are admired and approved of by a great number of other people – something that many teens seek for themselves.

It is through projection and identification that teens get into contact with those apparently superhuman qualities, and gradually discover that they themselves have some of those qualities within them.

Taking such processes seriously and selecting content in the form of stories that support teenagers' natural search for positive human qualities and values will lead to more emotional engagement and hence higher levels of motivation in otherwise reluctant students. In addition, it helps develop the students' own cognitive tools by encouraging them to understand that all human knowledge and achievement was once just a dream in someone's mind.

Teachers of teenage students frequently notice that it is difficult to get their students to talk about things that relate to themselves – this, in spite of the fact that teachers know that personalisation is an important tool for learning a foreign language successfully. Teens, however, don't often want to talk about themselves, and as their teachers or parents we have to accept that and try to gently guide them through this insecure stage. One way of doing that is using drama activities because they offer students rich opportunities to 'hide behind a character'. They know that their audience knows that what they are saying is not what they think, and that it is someone else's lines they are acting out.

So when teens act out a role they are not talking as themselves; yet the process of identification with the role makes it possible for them to develop a feeling of ownership during the period of rehearsing and acting out a play. The modern teen dramas in *Get on Stage!* are developed to do exactly that – they give students the opportunity to 'step out' of their own situation, and to experiment, reflect on and familiarise themselves with a variety of behaviours, attitudes and beliefs as they act as someone else, yet bring to that role their own thoughts and emotions.

The content of these plays makes it easy to grab students' attention, and consequently the content of the plays becomes more memorable. When students remember the content of a play well, the chances are that the language too will stick in their long-term memory better. And finally, good plays are far more likely to trigger responses from students, enlivening lessons and creating a more positive experience all round.

How to cast a play

Teachers casting a play are frequently torn between the crucial question of whether to choose the best actors for each role so that the drama comes fully alive, or whether to use the play as an educational tool where it isn't just the performance that counts (as a means of impressing the audience), but the process that leads up to the performance. It is important to keep in mind here that acting out a play is a holistic process where

Introduction

everyone taking part in it is very important to its success. The performance by a very shy student who finally manages to speak two lines in the play in a way that exceeds the student's own expectation of what they would ever be able to achieve may seem insignificant within the performance as such – but it might well be a massive step forward in the development of that particular student. You can be sure that the piece (whether a short sketch or a longer play) is written in such a way that it will work even if not every child in your class is a born actor. Most of the plays in *Get on Stage!* offer lots of opportunities for every child in your class to contribute to the play without feeling intimidated.

There are several options you can use if you want to cast a play:

1) **Let the individual students choose.**

    If you want to leave it to your students to choose what roles they want to play, you could work first on the comprehension of the script and do some language work with the worksheets at the end of the book, and then simply ask who would like to act out which role. This is a very 'democratic' process, but it may not be ideal for the shyer students, especially in an adolescent class. They may not want to step forward and ask for a role, much as they might like to be part of the cast. In this context, it would not be unusual for those students who tend to be more extrovert to get all the roles.

2) **The decisions are made by you.**

    Choosing the roles beforehand without asking your students allows you to find a match between what you think would be the right role for each of your students and what would be best for the performance in general.

    You can also use the performance of a play as an opportunity for your students to grow personally, by selecting students because you believe it would be good for their personal development. By telling a shy student 'I'd like you to play this part because I think you'll be good', you may be putting pressure on them – but this may be the gentle push needed by that student to make the next important step in their own development and hence be the right thing to do sometimes. On the other hand, you may feel that a student is not yet ready to appear on the stage. There is no point in forcing a student to take part in a performance if they are not at all keen. If you come across a student who refuses to play a role you have selected, it could be a good idea to ask them questions (in a non-judgemental way) about their reasons. It may then turn out that giving that student another task – whether it is about making props, being responsible for the lights during the performance or something else – is the right thing to go for, and this would be an entirely valid pedagogical decision, as that student can still contribute something useful and valuable to the success of the play.

    One way to involve a student linguistically without forcing them into performing is for them to act as 'prompt' during rehearsals and performances. This means they follow the script whilst the other students are rehearsing and, when a line is

Introduction

forgotten, they provide the prompt and read out the forgotten line. This task could be shared from rehearsal to rehearsal. Accepted protocol for this requires that the prompter only prompts when they hear the struggling actor say 'line' – this is in order to avoid a situation where an actor, pausing for dramatic effect, has their 'moment' ruined by an over-zealous prompter bellowing out the next line before being asked!

3) **Let the class decide.**

This third option is one that requires a fairly high level of maturity within your students. It will be suitable if you have a very good rapport with your class and, if the students themselves have a good rapport with each other – a classroom culture that usually needs to be developed. By showing your students that the selection process should not just be a matter of who makes themselves heard first and loudest when you ask who wants to play which role, the process of choosing roles can gradually become a valuable experience for your students in which they learn to make informed decisions and reflect on what are to become their rather than your choices.

You could start such a process by brainstorming criteria for the selection with your students, and writing them on the board, e.g. *Who **didn't** get a part the last time round when the class acted out a play? Who would you like to suggest for a role because you think it would be a good experience for **them**? Who has never had a part in a play?* etc. In order to avoid the more extrovert students always getting the roles they want, you could then ask students to write on a piece of paper which role they would like to play. One student collects all the names, and writes them alphabetically on the board – underneath the name of the character they want to act out. The choice is then up to the students, and they need to decide in group or whole-class discussions. This process will require more time, discipline and the ability to reflect on decision making and choice on the part of your students – but it is in itself a very valuable activity if carried out in the foreign language.

How to choose a play for your class

While you know best what kind of play is likely to be most suitable for your class, *Get on Stage!* gives you quite a bit of information about each one, supporting you in making appropriate choices. In the introduction for each play, you will find information about the estimated runtime, the props required, and the language level that a particular play is for. You will also see – indicated by the icons in the margin – whether there is an audio or video recording of the play you are thinking of choosing, and see thumbnails of the worksheets to aid comprehension and support the language work you are planning to do.

You will want to make yourself familiar with the content of the plays before choosing. You can use the synopses to pre-select the plays to shortlist for your class. The age of

Introduction

your students is another important criterion; younger students may love to act out a humorous sketch, while a teenage class may be keener on acting out a play based on a traditional story – or may prefer the dramatic, soap-opera-like quality of one of the modern teen plays, with the dilemmas they present. If you teach a rather buoyant class you may want to pick a more serious piece in order to get them into a more reflective mood. If you have a quiet class, you may want to pick a more humorous piece that helps to bring the fun out in your students and raise the energy level in your class. Again, depending on the level of maturity of your students, you may decide to involve them in the decision-making process. You could, for example, give them photocopies of several plays to read and choose from, or you could read out the synopses of various plays and ask them for their preferences. Thinking about which play they themselves would love to do most and which would be best for the audience is valuable practice in thinking ahead. Seeing the play through the eyes of whoever the audience is going to be helps develop students' empathic skills.

Introduction

Physical Warm-Up Games

Warming up physically before a drama session or rehearsal not only prepares the body for the physical rigours ahead but also gets the blood pumping to the brain allowing better concentration and mental application. A set pattern of physical stretches that warms up each part of the body also allows messages between the brain and the body to travel more efficiently and can also ease students away from the world of jumbled thoughts they arrived with and into the world of the rehearsal room. The stretches you use can be the same as those for a sports warm-up but don't allow students to push themselves too much as it is a drama class we are preparing for and not a pole vault. It is advisable to keep these warm-up stretch routines exactly the same each time as the very repetition and familiarity allows students to find the right mental state in which to rehearse. Having said that, it is always fun to add a few physical games to vary the routine and keep the mood buoyant. Here are a few suggestions. Some require both physical and mental stamina.

Points of the Compass

Designate each side of the room as points on the compass, North, South, East and West. When you shout a point the students must run to it.

Variations:
- around the world – run clockwise around the room;
- end of the world – play dead.

Port and Starboard

The sides of room become parts of a ship, Port, Starboard, bow, stern. You call – pupils run.

Variations:
- man overboard – run to the sides;
- man the rigging – pretend to climb;
- scrub the deck – pretend to scrub;
- hit the deck – play dead.

Cat and Mouse

Every student has a partner and hold hands (or wrists) except two students who remain un-attached. Designate one as the cat and one as the mouse. The cat chases the mouse but the mouse, if they wish, can escape by holding the hand/wrist of someone who is already in a couple. The person in the couple whose hand isn't being held becomes

Introduction

the mouse so has to let go of his/her partner's hand and try to escape the cat. If the cat does catch the mouse they can swap roles.

Good Morning

Each student has to say 'Good morning' and shake the hands of all the other students while keeping the other hand shaking someone else's hand – only when both hands are occupied in handshaking can the student disengage and find someone else.

Blob

Students spread out in a defined area. One student is chosen as 'The Blob'. At the teacher's command 'The Blob' tries to tag (i.e. touch) the others. Once a person is tagged they attach themselves to 'The Blob' and become part of it. This continues until everyone is part of 'The Blob'. Encourage students to attach themselves in ways other than simply holding hands, the more 'Blob'-like the creature becomes, the more fun.

Once the game is over play it again but emphasise the teamwork and co-operation aspects and encourage your students to discuss tactics that will help when hunting as 'The Blob' or trying to avoid being assimilated by 'The Blob'. This will also move focus away from who was 'The Winner' and who was 'The Loser'.

Variation
The same as above but with everyone blindfolded. Stress the importance of moving slowly and stealthily and encourage your students to start relying on senses other than sight alone as they hunt or attempt avoidance. Once everyone is blindfold, touch your 'Blob' on the shoulder and then give the command for the game to start. As people feel themselves being tagged they silently join 'The Blob'.

Silent Terror or Snake in the Dark

Another slight variation on 'The Blob'. Spread your students out around the space and ask them to close their eyes. Then ask them to walk around the room with eyes shut. Select one student to be the snake or 'The Silent Terror'. They try to catch the others. If they are the snake they must hiss so that their prey can listen and try to avoid them. If they are the 'The Silent Terror', they make no sound at all but the others must whisper 'Silent Terror' whenever they touch someone else. If there is no reply then they have been caught by the Silent Terror. The person who is caught must join the back of the monster (hold onto waist of the last caught person). If the monster is the snake, victims must join the back when they have been hissed at!

Introduction

Handkerchief

Each player has a piece of material tucked in the top of the back of his or her trousers or skirt but with one piece clearly visible. The object of the game is for each player to collect as many of the other players' 'handkerchiefs' without having his or her own taken.

Keepie Uppie

The group has to keep a soft ball in the air for as many touches as possible. Each player is only allowed to touch it once in succession. If it touches the floor, or if any player takes more than one touch, the game must start again from number one. By using a balloon you make the game much easier but it means you can add further rules – such as using only feet and heads, left hand only, and so on.

Steer Me!

Each student takes a partner and they take it in turns to safely manoeuvre each other around the space but the student being steered is blindfold. They are not allowed to speak, and each pair should develop their own series of physical commands, for example tapping on the left shoulder to turn left. We recommend deciding on a 'stop' signal before all others! Students will be surprised at the level of trust they can develop in their partners as they are steered around a busy room. As confidence grows, increase the speed.

Oh! What a Tangled Web We Weave!

Students form a standing circle and hold hands. Split the group in the middle. One end begins to weave through the arms and legs of the rest of the group. Shout, 'Freeze!' – the two lines must untangle themselves without letting go of each other's hands and then reform the circle.

Zombie

This game works best if your students know each other's names at least reasonably well. They all stand in a well-spaced circle. Designate one to be 'Zombie'. That student puts their arms out in front of them and walks slowly, like a zombie, across the circle toward someone roughly opposite. The person being stalked needs to catch the eye of someone else in the circle who will then release them by calling their name (the name of the person being stalked, not their own!). The person who was being stalked by the zombie then becomes the zombie and sets off towards the person who released them whilst the original zombie takes their place in the circle. The person now being stalked has, in turn, to catch the eye of someone else in the circle to release them. This game

Introduction

is excellent for concentration as it only works efficiently when the students realize that the best method for success is to remain calm and focused and in tune with each other. Essential for drama! If the zombie catches the person before they are released, you can decide that they are 'out' or you can decide that the person who failed to release them in time is 'out' but until the pattern is established and the hysteria has subsided it's best to keep all involved.

Fruit Salad

Sit the students on chairs in a circle and give each student the name of a fruit making sure there are at least two of each fruit. When their fruit is called, they must change seats. The rules are:
- students cannot return to their original seat
- students cannot sit in seats to the immediate right and left of their own seat.

Variations

Choose categories other than fruit: animals, cities, famous people, insects, numbers.

Anyone Who …

Arrange a circle of chairs but with one less chair than you have students. Everyone sits except one person who stands in the middle. That person then makes the statement 'Anyone who …' and completes it with a category of their choice, 'has blonde hair …', 'likes Hip-Hop …'. Any students who feel that description fits them have to swap seats with each other whilst the original questioner tries to sit in a vacated chair. Whoever is left without a chair becomes the questioner.

The L-shaped Walk

Everyone finds a space and stands still. The only way to move around the room is in an L shape – 2 steps, a right-angled turn, then 3 steps or 3 steps, a right-angled turn and then 2 steps. Explain that the students must not touch anyone else and must pause if they are going to bump into others. Students move on the teacher's command.

Variations:
- alter pace (fast or slow), direction, mood, eyes shut.
- move to spot – choose a spot in the room, fix your eyes upon it, now move towards it without touching anyone on the way. (Vary pace, back/forward, eyes shut and so on.)

Introduction

Tips and guidelines for staging and performing a play

Voice projection

....

Basic message to get across to your students:
Remember: you're performing for the audience, and not for each other.

....

One of the most difficult ideas to get across to a student actor and even some adult actors is the absolute need for every member of the audience to hear what they are saying. No matter how brilliantly they are acting, if the audience can't hear them they disengage and become bored, restless and even angry. But voice projection isn't easy, particularly for teenagers whose voices are still in physical development, and whose self-confidence levels may not support the idea of expressing themselves loudly. However, we've all experienced the situation where before a rehearsal or lesson starts a group of kids can generate ear-splitting levels of noise, but after the start their voices seem to magically disappear when they're asked to contribute formally.

It can take years to train a voice properly, but the following tips will help maximise the vocal potential of your student actors in a rather shorter time.

1) **Seeing is hearing**

   If the audience can *see* an actor's mouth then they can hear better. Sounds odd, but is perfectly true – so encourage your actors to keep their heads up, and even when two characters are talking directly to each other they should try and share the scene with the audience (see also 'Backs are bad' on the following page).

2) **Throw your voice**

   Get your students to imagine they're throwing their voices up and over the audience so that it lands on the back row. This avoids a natural tendency for actors to perform only for the front two rows and ignore the rest of the audience, which in turn means they underestimate the volume required. A really good exercise to make this tangible for your students is to split the cast into two groups; whilst half of them stay in the performance space the other half stand where the back row of the audience will be, and then you get them to rehearse the play across that divide. They will soon become aware of the volume required to hear each other and therefore the volume required for the audience to hear them in performance.

3) **A column of sound**

   The voice should come from the pit of the stomach, not the throat. This reduces the danger of straining the vocal chords and produces greater volume. To get your students to understand this, ask them to do a deep belly laugh – Ha, ha, ha, ha, ha! whilst placing their hand on their stomach, and then ask them to concentrate on the feeling of the stomach muscles. They will experience the sound in their throats as well, but encourage them to focus on getting more and more of the sound to start from the stomach. Stress the need for them to keep the throat relaxed and

Introduction

open. Then get them to say one line at a time, asking them to visualise the line starting in the pit of the stomach and then rising as a continuous column of sound up through the body, out of the mouth and right over to the back of the audience.

4) Keep breathing!

It may seem simplistic, but one of the most important rules of acting is 'keep breathing!'. Often, the tension involved in rehearsing and performing makes us forget this most basic of rules. Make sure your students take a deep enough breath to get them through the line so that the end of the line is as well supported as the beginning, and the volume won't tail off into inaudibility.

5) Not the Opera House!

Make absolutely sure you choose your performance space wisely. It's not going to work if you rehearse your play in a classroom and, encouraged by the results, book the nearest opera house for your performance. Be realistic about how large a space can be managed vocally by your students. It's vital for their confidence that they don't feel overawed by the challenge of filling too large a physical space.

Staging and 'blocking'

Basic message to get across to your students:
Remember the audience

Although this may seem an obvious point to make, it is worth asking your students on a regular basis, 'Where is the audience?' By doing this repeatedly, you will gradually allow the students to develop the actor's instinct of being constantly aware that they are performing not for each other but for an external entity, 'the Audience'. This may simply be classmates if the performance is to be in the classroom, or an actual audience of other classes, parents, friends and family if you have prepared a play to perform in a larger space – but the same rules apply.

1) Backs are bad/Upstaging

Unless you are creating a specific dramatic effect, an audience will not want to see the actors' backs, as this creates a barrier between the audience and the story. When you plan the characters' moves (this is what 'blocking' is), make sure that their faces are always seen, whether talking or reacting to what is happening, as that is far more engaging than the sight of someone's back.

However, sometimes you may deliberately use backs as an effect – when, for instance, you want the audience to focus on two characters in a crowd scene. In our play *Friendship* (pp 172–181) there is a party scene where we have prescribed that the audience should only see the faces of Lisa and Sheri, with the other characters at the party keeping their backs to the audience, who can then concentrate on the reactions of the two featured characters; but this example is the exception rather than the rule.

Introduction

Upstaging is a term used to describe what happens when an actor in a scene stands too far towards the back of the stage compared to the other actors. This forces them to turn their backs on the audience in order to speak to the 'upstaging' actor, and as mentioned above ... backs are not what an audience wants.

2) NOT straight lines

Even professional actors have a strange desire to stand in a straight line when a few of them find themselves on stage together, but it looks terribly boring from the audience's point of view. Unless your cast are going to dance the can-can, encourage them to stagger a straight line. However, be careful they don't 'upstage' each other.

3) Back foot, front foot

This is a difficult idea to describe but a simple idea to enact, so please watch the section on the DVD if you are not sure what we mean. Essentially what it entails is that if two actors or more are acting out a dialogue, then the actor whose turn it is to speak takes a small step backwards and shifts their weight onto their back foot. This turns their body towards the audience and slightly away from the other actor(s), helping the audience see their face when they're speaking. When the line is finished, the actor turns back again towards whoever has the next line, taking a small step forwards.

4) Sight lines

The lines of vision from the audience to the stage are called 'sight lines'. When you know where you are performing and you know where your audience will be seated, do the best you can to ensure that whoever sits in the seats at the ends of the rows can see **all** the actors on stage **all** of the time; if Jimmy's grandma is sitting at the end of a row A and she can't see Jimmy because other actors keep standing between her and her beloved grandson, then she won't be happy. To help with this problem, make sure that your first row of audience seating isn't too close to the stage. Also, don't let the characters on stage stand too close together, as this closes down what the audience can see; don't bunch your actors like bananas!

5) Here I am! Here I go!

When making entrances and exits, the actors shouldn't physically 'apologise' for arriving on stage or leaving it.

Introduction

What helps avoid this happening is the actor knowing exactly why their character is entering the scene or leaving it. So, early in the rehearsal schedule ask your actors 'Why is your character here, and what does he/she want?' and 'Why is your character leaving? Where are they going?' It may be that their character is timid and should indeed apologise physically for entering and exiting – but that then becomes a creative choice rather than an insecure actor's choice.

6) **Levels**

Choose your performance space so that even audience members in the back row can see as much as possible of all the actors; audience members who have to strain to see soon lose interest. If you are performing in a hall and it has no stage, try and build up the acting area with rostrums.

Introducing levels on the stage itself can not only help with sightlines but can also add interest visually; for instance, simply adding a chair to a scene allows one character to sit and one to stand – or even stand on the chair!

7) **Movements and memory**

The most common question asked of professional actors is 'How do you remember your lines?' Well, one of the reasons the lines gradually sink in is that the brain's physical memory comes into play, and with repeated rehearsal the brain starts to be able to associate certain lines with certain movements. This means that in terms of learning lines, the actors' movements – both their gestures and their actual movements around the stage – are very important.

8) **What did I do last time?**

But before the physical memory has firmly taken hold, it's highly advisable to get your actors to pencil their moves into their scripts next to the appropriate line. We say 'pencil' because you may decide to change a move as rehearsals develop. Elsewhere in this introduction (see 9) below) we refer to the advantages to be gained by having someone else – maybe a member of the class who is reluctant to perform but still wants to be involved – to keep an independent record of all the moves in a separate script. The main advantage of requiring all the moves to be written down is that it saves considerable time being wasted in rehearsal as the actors try to remember what they did last time.

9) **Blocking**

The movements that the actors make around the stage during a play which have been devised during rehearsals are known collectively as the 'blocking' and another vital task the reluctant actors in your class can perform during rehearsals is to write the 'blocking' down so that you have a ready record from rehearsal to rehearsal of what was done previously – this saves a lot of time and argument! The easiest way to do this is by having a photocopied page of script in a ring-binder with a blank sheet of paper opposite and every move is written on the blank sheet of paper in the form of a diagram with a line drawn across to the particular word/phrase with which it is associated. For instance, if your setting had two chairs and a table and an

Introduction

actor moved from one chair to the other whilst saying 'I need to be able to see out of the window' you would draw a very simple bird's eye view of the chairs and table with the actor's initials in the chair from which they move and an arrow across to the other chair and then a line is drawn from that diagram across to the line in the script. This, again, keeps the student responsible fully involved with the text without having to perform.

The following diagram shows an example of how the actors' moves can be recorded in a ring binder. It's from the play *Being Polite* (p 56–61) which is also available on the DVD. As you can see, the notes contain abbreviations (SK = Shopkeeper, SA1 = Shop assistant 1, SA2 = Shop assistant 2, C1 = Customer 1 and C2 = Customer 2). The rectangles represent the two sales counters.

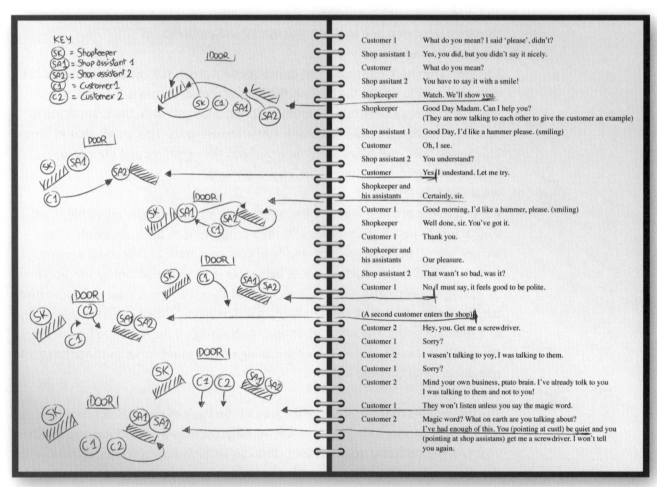

The actors movements are jotted down on the left.   *The script sequences are on the right with the drawn pencil lines matching up.*

Introduction

Concentration and focus

....

Basic message to get across to your students:
Support Each Other!

....

This section deals with one of the most important aspects of staging a play; 'focus' means the audience's attention being concentrated on where it needs to be at any given time. *VITAL!*
So here is a list of those aspects:

1) **Don't fiddle!**
Assuming that Sally is playing a character called Kate, you need to stress to your students that when Kate isn't speaking Sally mustn't fiddle with her hair, look out to see where Mum is sitting, yawn, keep scratching her head, have a giggle with another actor next to her – whatever! – as no matter how good the other actors are, the audience – guaranteed! – will become riveted by Sally's dandruff or intrigued by what's making her giggle, and not stay focused on the world of the play where Kate exists.

2) **Mirroring**
When any actor is on stage but not actively saying their lines, their job is to focus audience attention onto the person who is speaking. This means that should audience attention drift away from the main action, the supporting actors will immediately redirect it back again. The simplest way for you as a director to achieve this is to make sure every eye on stage is looking towards where you want the audience to look; the supporting actors are working as a mirror.
There may, however, be the odd exception – if, for instance, a character is meant to be bored by what is being said, then they will probably not want to focus on the action – but this will have been dictated by the demands of character or situation within the play.

3) **Listen, and be 'in the moment'**
No matter how many times the actors have rehearsed a play, the audience are seeing it for the first time, so it is important for the actors to be 'in the moment'. This means they shouldn't anticipate what is going to happen, even though they know because they've rehearsed it twenty times. The best way for the actors to do this is very simple: they should keep listening, particularly when they are performing in a language that is not their native tongue. By listening, they can avoid a situation such as this one: a sound cue is late and the actor isn't really listening, so he picks up the phone before it has even rung and says, 'David Walters here; who's that?' He has reacted to a sound that didn't happen in that performance, and he did this because it had always happened in rehearsals. Another reason for actors to be in the moment is that if actor A is listening when actor B forgets their lines, A might be able to help B out.

Introduction

If something does go wrong, there are usually two outcomes: either the audience don't notice, unless the actors make it obvious something has gone wrong by coming out of character or coming out of the world of the play – or the audience do notice. In which case the actors should do the opposite …

4) **If it itches, scratch it!**
If Sally needs to sneeze, for example, then she can sneeze – but sneeze as Kate, staying in character. This means that if the audience are tempted to giggle they look at Sally but see Kate – still in character, still focused on the play – and they soon forget it ever happened. A straightforward sneeze is a lot less distracting than watching Sally spend 60 seconds or more trying desperately to stifle a sneeze. So whatever the actors need to do, they can do it – but they must stay in character.

5) **Enjoy it, relax … nothing can go wrong!**
If something goes disastrously wrong and it's obvious the audience have noticed, then the actors should just relax and let the audience know that they too know it's gone wrong.

If the audience know something has gone wrong, they are going to be worried and even embarrassed for the actors – but if the actors let the audience know that they don't really mind, then the audience can relax and actually enjoy the moment with the actors. In a comedy, some of the finest moments can be when something goes wrong – provided the actors share it with the audience, who will suddenly feel really part of it. If an actor passes a cup to another actor and they drop it, the audience will worry – but the first actor turns to them and ad-libs, saying directly to them, 'I told him he needed glasses!' the audience will relax and laugh really loudly.

6) **Staying in character: acting is also reacting**
Make sure your actors stay in character throughout; one of the easiest ways of losing audience focus is when an actor, having said their line, goes back to being himself or herself whilst others speak. This is because when a line is spoken, the audience will be interested not only in what was said but also in how other characters on stage react to the line. To continue with Sally and her character Kate, if Kate angrily asks another character, 'What did you mean by that?', but Sally goes back to being herself whilst the other character explains, then the audience will become confused. Kate has to be onstage for the duration of the play, and Sally can only come back when the play has ended.

7) **Don't tread on a laugh**
A common trap fallen into by the inexperienced actor when performing comedy is 'treading on a laugh'. This phrase refers to the situation where the audience laugh at a line or situation in a play but the actor with the next line proceeds to deliver that line whilst the audience is still laughing and as a consequence the line gets lost. This line might be a vital piece of plot information or a line designed to get yet another laugh but will fail to have the designed effect if it is lost in uproarious audience mirth! If the audience do laugh then tell your actors to stay in character

Introduction

and enjoy the laugh but simply wait until the laugh has subsided enough for the next line to be heard. The fact that the audience will know you are waiting for them will greatly empower them and allow them to feel really part of the experience. Prepare your actors to be ready for laughs BUT not to take them for granted. There's nothing worse than an actor waiting for an anticipated laugh that fails to arrive. The other side to that coin is that in every comedy you will find lines that you consider mundane to be inexplicably hilarious to your audience.

Interestingly, performing comedy for an audience in a language other than their native tongue creates one unique situation and that is the 'double-laugh'. The 'double-laugh' is what happens when part of the audience whose comprehension is high laugh immediately but then have to take a moment to explain the joke to others in the audience whose comprehension is less advanced who then laugh themselves. Knowing when to wait for the 'double-laugh' cannot be taught but comes only with experience; however if the concept is explained it can help!

Building the characters to tell your story

Basic message to get across to your students:
Do it physically!

Although the primary purpose of *Get on Stage!* is to allow the English language to be practised and used by students in a hopefully engaging way, the overall enjoyment of the experience is greatly enhanced by allowing them to experiment physically with the characters. Physicality can really help to tell a story. When a character shuffles onto the stage, bent over and using a walking stick, then even before they've said a word the audience know they are old, so that they can immediately focus on what the character is going to say. Also, by a character having obvious physical attributes, the less secure students can hide behind these and feel free to experiment, as it's not them but the character who is doing everything.

1) **Gesture**

   Sometimes (particularly, though not exclusively, for comedy purposes), an actor may put in an exaggerated gesture for emphasis. This can not only help the comedy, but also associating a gesture with a word can help as a memory aid for the actor – remember the point made earlier about the brain's 'physical memory'? In the play *Being Polite* on the DVD, there is a demonstration of gestures being used for comic effect when the characters say 'magic word' and 'please'.

2) **How does my character stand and walk?**

   Once you have decided on a play, ask your students to stand and walk in the way they think the various characters should stand and walk: a handsome prince, an old woman, a policeman …

Introduction

3) Who does my character remind me of?
Sometimes it helps to ask your students to think of someone they know, either from their own lives or fictional characters who remind them, if only a bit, of the character they are going to play. That gives the inexperienced actors a useful starting point, for both voice and movements.

4) Hands
Believe it or not, one of the hardest things about acting is to know what to do with your hands. What you don't want is a stage full of actors with their hands thrust deep into pockets because they don't know what to do with them. Another trap is that actors can overuse their hands by emphasising every word with a gesture. So tell the students that if in doubt they can let their hands hang by their sides; it's fine.

However, hands can be used to great effect if used properly. Suggest some emotional and physical states and ask your actors to come up with suitable hand actions such as these:

- exasperated – hands on head pulling own hair
- thinking – one arm folded across the chest, the other stroking the chin
- angry – arms held rigidly at the sides of the body, hands making tight fists
- cold – the character blows on their hands
- hot – the character fans their face with their hand.

And if one character fans their face but the other characters don't, the audience will know that that character has been running or exerting themselves.
All these physical signals help an audience prepare for the language, so that even if they don't understand every word they can get the general idea.

5) There's no such thing as a small part
Encourage your students to approach playing the smaller parts with as much care as the bigger parts. In Shakespeare's *Macbeth*, there is a character, Seyton, who only has two lines but if he doesn't come on and tell Macbeth that his wife is dead, then the rest of the play can't happen at all. And if the actor playing Seyton doesn't project the right sense of fear for what he is about to say, but instead, casually and chewing gum, mentions the fact that the queen is dead, then the whole play is ruined. *There is no such thing as a small part.* For example, in some of the plays in *Get on Stage!* there are characters described simply as customers – but if each customer is thought about and turned into an individual, then the play becomes much more satisfying overall for both cast and audience.

So, ask the students to find a word they think describes some aspect of their character, then ask them to look that word up in a thesaurus – and they will discover all sorts of subtle differences in the way they can act out the original word.

Introduction

Pace

Basic message to get across to your students:
Slow, slow – quick, quick, slow

'Pace' is a word that is often misinterpreted by actors as meaning 'fast' – but in fact, just as in sport, pace describes the speed at which a scene or play should be played, be it fast, slow, steady, frantic etc. By varying the pace of a scene an entirely different effect can be achieved. There have been occasions when we have been struggling to define what exactly is wrong with a particular scene, and then we have discovered that just by either speeding up the pace or slowing it down all the problems disappear and the scene comes into focus. Within a play there may, depending on the narrative, be many differently paced scenes.

Here are some ways in which the appropriate pace can be achieved:

1) Picking up cues

This phrase means 'don't leave unjustified pauses between the lines'. In our short play *Smart Shoppers* (pp 40–42) there is a section of dialogue as follows:

Woman	(*twirling around*) Well? How do I look in my new dress?
Man	You look marvellous, darling. Happy anniversary.
Woman	You're sure it doesn't make my bottom look a bit fat?
Man	Not at all. But ...
Woman	(*alarmed*) What? What's the matter? I look awful, don't I?
Man	Calm down, darling – there's nothing wrong! It's just that you look so lovely in that dress I want to get you something else to match.

Taking a real-life situation, if after a woman has said 'I look awful, don't I?' a man were to pause before responding, then the woman would probably carry on talking, asking him further questions and getting more desperate – but those lines aren't in the script, so it's essential for the actor playing Man to pick up his cue and respond immediately with his 'Calm down, darling'.

In addition, Man, by picking up his cue promptly, can then relax and slow down his pace throughout the rest of his speech, just as he would if he really were trying to calm her down.

Important! Picking up a cue doesn't mean the actor can gabble their next line; it just means that unwarranted gaps in the dialogue are avoided, and so the play feels fast and interesting, but remains completely understandable.

2) Don't let your character pick up another character's pace

Referring to the above extract again, Man must be careful not to pick up the pace of Woman's 'I look awful'. Her speech is to be made in an alarmed and even hasty manner – but Man must in contrast speak slowly, calmly and reassuringly. It may

Introduction

seem a rather obvious point to make, but when adrenalin is involved it is easy for every actor to unwittingly follow the pace of the previous speech, be it fast or slow, and this leads to one-dimensional performances that are either way too fast or way too slow.

3) Don't rush through the 'boring bits'/Remember the audience have never heard it before

Another trap is the actors forgetting that although they may have rehearsed and rehearsed and rehearsed a play, an audience is seeing it for the first time. So in the final rehearsals, don't let them rush through bits they know really well or think might have got a bit boring. It's true that some parts of a play may come together really quickly, and the actors may get a bit bored and want to get onto the bit they really enjoy – but as often as not the audience really need to hear and understand the 'boring' bit in order to make sense of the 'exciting' bit.

4) Emphasis and repetition

Sometimes a line in a playscript will be repeated, and varying the pace and emphasis of the repeats allows you to create completely different effects. For instance, imagine a character has to repeat three times the line, 'He said I'm a monkey face!'

- If the character says it the first time quietly and slowly, and gets louder and faster on each repeat, this can indicate that he/she may have started shocked or quietly seething, and ended up in a towering rage, implying the unwritten line 'And I'm going to *get him!*'
- However, if the character says it the first time loudly, quickly and angrily, and gradually gets quieter and slower, then they may have gradually got more upset and sad, implying the unwritten line 'And I'm really hurt.'

So, varying the pace is a useful tool for creating dramatic interest. Play with it!

Set, props, lights, music and sound effects

Basic message to get across to your students:
Do It Yourself!

Each individual play in this book gives you guidance, but here are a few general points.

1) Set

The plays in *Get on Stage!* do not rely on elaborate sets. They can all be made with tables and chairs and other easily obtainable objects. Part of the fun is finding simple ways to create a set; if in doubt, paint it and stick it up! Remember, a desk is a desk until you add a paper tablecloth and a paper rose … when it becomes part of a posh restaurant. Or a table put up on a small platform with a paper sign saying 'Fast Food' and two painted wheels stuck on the audience side of the platform

Introduction

becomes a fast-food van – your audience's imagination will do the rest. The DVD version of *Rusty Nail Soup* (p 127) demonstrates how to create an environment using the actors themselves as doors and cupboards.

This doesn't mean you shouldn't be as creative as you wish and build whatever you want – but equally, if you haven't got the resources or time to build anything at all, then just get a student to read out the set descriptions and stage directions, and allow the audience to create the world for themselves. That in itself will create a special magic.

If you do build anything, then make sure that it is safe and 'excited-kid-proof'. Clip the tablecloth to the desk and blu-tack the vase to the cloth, so that if your young actors, in their excitement, leap up from the restaurant table they don't take everything with them. Because despite earlier messages saying nothing can go wrong, there's no point in going looking for trouble; performing a play is quite nerve-racking enough for your actors without them wondering if a piece of wobbly scenery is about to crash down on their heads!

2) **Props**

The same rules apply as above; simple and safe. If an actor comes on stage with a broom handle and tells the audience it's a laser gun, they'll believe it.

3) **Lights**

If you can get hold of some simple lighting then that's great because it can help define the performance area and create a sense of occasion. But no way are they essential – Shakespeare only had a few candles and he managed. Dimming the lights between scenes is a simple and effective way of denoting the passing of time or a change in location, particularly if accompanied by music (see below). If you do decide to use lighting take time to focus the lighting on the areas of the stage where the action will occur. Sounds obvious but the audience's eyes will be drawn to the brightest spots on the stage so if you have a chair onstage and a character sits on that chair make sure the light hits the chair and mark the floor of the stage with tape so you know where the chair is meant to be every time you perform.

A light focused on the wrong spot can be terribly distracting as the audience start to think 'I wonder what's going to happen in that bright patch of light?' rather than concentrating on the play as it unfolds.

4) **Music**

Music, with or without lighting, is an incredibly useful method of setting or changing the emotional texture of a scene. You will struggle to watch a film or TV show where music is *not* used as an amazingly effective shortcut to tell the audience what they should be feeling. If your class is blessed with students who can play an instrument, then so much the better! A simple tune played on the recorder can be used to suggest a variety of different moods. A Scottish lament can invoke terrible sadness and yearning whereas a jaunty Scottish reel cannot fail to bring a smile. Any of the short comedy sketches in *Get on Stage!* would benefit greatly by

Introduction

having kazoos played before and after each scene. (Kazoos are brilliant for comedy as they require no instrumental ability whatsoever and are inherently 'silly'.) Music can allow an audience to know where they are before a word has been spoken, so that they can immediately attune to the dialogue. Even without the luxury of live music, existing music/songs played on CD are just fine and allow students to really think about a play and suggest which of their favourite songs/tunes might fit.

5) Sound effects

The Internet is full of sites where you can download simple sound effects to help create an atmosphere or mark a particular moment, and most cheap keyboards contain a bewildering variety of bleeps and bongs that can be easily utilised for a show. But it's far better, in our opinion, if the students create their own sound effects with their own voices. *Rusty Nail Soup* (p 127) on the DVD uses the actors to create a creaky door and a slamming one, both physically and vocally, which is more satisfying in a theatrical sense. Also, some of the playscripts in *Get on Stage!* contain specific suggestions for vocal sound effects, but we're sure you will be able to find opportunities that we've missed!

Changing scenes

Basic message to get across to your students:
Make sure your audience knows what you know!

In a big theatre scene changes are easily marked by a number of things, for example curtains falling and rising, a change in the lights (e.g. from day to night time), or a different setting specified through different props. None of these may be available for your performance. However, possible changes in time and location have to be made clear to the audience in order for them to be able to follow the play.

A number of the plays in this book have been written in such a way that the scene change follows naturally from what is said by the actors or the narrator(s).

In *The Children and the Wind*, for example, there is a chicken who acts as a narrator. Whenever a scene change happens, the chicken announces that as part of her narration. When at the end of the first scene, for example, Mum wants to make some pancakes for the children, but she doesn't have any flour, and the children decide to go to the miller to get some, the chicken says:

CHICKEN   And off they went to the miller, where they filled their bowl with flour. They were very happy, but as they walked back, dreaming of pancakes, something happened.

This makes it clear to the audience that the next scene is set outside the flour mill and it might not be necessary to further indicate that there has been a change of scene.

Introduction

If you want to be on the safe side, however, it might be advantageous to indicate the change of scene also visually, for example by getting a student to walk across the stage holding a board with the new scene written on, clearly visible to everyone in the audience.

An alternative way of communicating changes of scene visually to the audience would be for a pair of students to carry in a flip chart where the different stage settings have been written beforehand, one page per scene. The students enter, put down the flipchart, turn the page so the audience can see the specifications for the next scene, and point at it, pausing a bit to give the audience time to read what's on the flip chart.

As we have stressed, visual announcements give clear indications to the audience and should therefore be used routinely when you get your students to perform a play. The other advantage of using them lies in the fact that you can involve more students in the performance.

 ## Remembering or learning lines

Basic message to get across to your students:
Moving Makes Memories!

'How do you remember your lines?' This is the *wrong* question to ask your students!

'How do you *learn* your lines?' is more to the point.

A line will stubbornly refuse to be remembered until it has been properly learnt. So, what does 'properly learnt' mean? There are three parts to it, and they apply to all of us:

- Intellectual Memory
  This is the part of the line-learning process when our brain reads the script and makes sense of each line, constructing a **logical progression** to help us remember it.
- Physical Memory
  Again, develops during rehearsals as the brain starts to associate **physical action** – sitting, standing, walking, handing over something, shaking our finger at someone – with each line.
- Emotional Memory
  Develops during rehearsals when the brain starts to remember **how we felt** when we spoke that line.

All three are equally important, but as we get older we rely more and more on emotional and physical memory, as the talent we innately have as young children to read something a couple of times and simply remember it starts to fade.

Introduction

Line learning depends crucially on understanding what each line means. That may sound obvious, but we have witnessed actors run through an entire part from memory yet still stumble over the same line over and over again – and the reason is always that they still don't really know *why* they're saying it!

So, here's a learning system we've found works well on the whole:

1) **Read**

   To begin with, the cast should read the play a number of times out loud to each other, so they start to understand it as a whole. Reading out loud is an entirely different exercise from reading quietly to oneself – it's a far more valuable one for this purpose, as it allows the brain to immediately start remembering how it physically feels to form and speak those particular words in that particular order and to make associations with the 'feel' of each line.

2) **Block**

   Then start to 'block' the play (i.e. direct the students' moves around the stage) so that their brains can associate their movements, gestures and other physical actions with the lines. Write the moves down in your script as an *aide-memoire*.

3) **Discuss**

   Discuss with the students what each line means and how their character feels when they say the line, so that each line has real thought behind it. This applies as much to silly comedy as to more serious material.

4) **Record**

   It's really useful to sound-record the play as soon as possible – you can do this with the actors reading their parts aloud – and then give each actor a copy of the recording so that they can speak along with it when they're away from rehearsals. Whenever they get an odd free moment they can turn on their mp3 player and practise; even just listening like this helps enormously, especially if the listener follows the lines in the script, as this starts them associating the sound of the lines with a 'picture' of them. It's amazing how quickly actors can tell you whereabouts on the page a line is, even if they can't quite remember the line itself with total accuracy.

   Listening to the recording as they go to sleep, too, is really helpful, as the brain has the ability to carry on working whilst one is asleep.

   Recording also allows each actor to get used to their fellow actors' voices.

   Sometimes an actor might like to record themselves doing all the parts except their own, leaving gaps where their character speaks.

5) **Repeat after me …**

   The scariest moment in rehearsals is when an actor has to put the script down and start remembering their lines rather than read them. So the earlier you get your students to face this the better, and you can do this by having someone 'feed' each actor their lines. Sometimes in rehearsals we won't let the actors have the scripts in their hands at all, but we feed them the lines and they repeat what they've heard.

Introduction

They can still use their recording and script when they practise on their own – but our method means that from the earliest possible point in time the actors can listen and react to each other, and won't ever have to face the dreadful moment when their accustomed safety blanket, the script, is taken away!

6) **Write**

A really simple exercise to test the memory is for the actor to write down their lines as they remember them, and then compare them with the script. This enables them to gauge where they need to concentrate their efforts.

7) **Relax**

Often an actor *will* know their lines but will *think* that they don't. It's part of the director's job to get them to relax and so allow their brain to access their memory stores without panic getting in the way.

And finally ...

....

Basic message to get across to your students:
Have Fun!

....

1) **There's no such thing as a Bad Actor**

Putting on a show only works as an entirely co-operative and mutually supportive venture. Some people are naturally more gifted actors than others, but if we assume that everyone is doing their best and will only get better with support and worse with criticism, then we won't go far wrong. *The experience must be fun so whilst we should encourage our young actors to be brave and fulfil their potential let's not ask for too much and spoil the fun.*

2) **There's no such thing as a Bad Idea**

The team effort required to stage a play is best achieved when everyone encourages each other to express themselves and their ideas. What may appear as a bad idea at first may trigger a train of thought and discussion that leads to a good idea. Even an idea that appears bad is better than no idea.

That said, you will need to introduce some form of discipline to control your free-for-all ideas sessions, so that those with the loudest voices and biggest personalities don't swamp those who are more reticent – but teachers know more about achieving that than most people do.

3) **Enjoy it. Relax. Nothing can go wrong!**

It's worth finishing off by repeating this core maxim:
If your students are enjoying it, the audience will enjoy it.
If your students are relaxed but excited, the audience will be relaxed but excited.
Nothing can go wrong ... even if it does!

Break a leg!!

Chapter 1
Short sketches

Short sketches

The Perfect Son

 ## A sketch in 1 scene

Roles	2–5 (the latter if the 'Person 2' role is shared between 2, 3 or even 4 actors)
Runtime	2 minutes, depending on production
Set	A park bench
Props	2 chairs or a bench optional: trees, bushes etc. – either represented by students, or made of cardboard, paper, wool
Style	A short, simple comedy sketch
Synopsis	A man brags to his friend he has the perfect son. The friend can't believe what he's hearing!
Language level	Elementary – A2
Language areas	Present simple (3rd person singular affirmative, negative and questions); verb phrases (*do homework, tell a lie, come home late* etc.)
Stage tips	This is a very simple sketch that doesn't require a lot of props. The scene can be set by using a few pictures of trees and bushes drawn on poster paper, and two chairs can be used as the park bench where the two people are sitting. Alternatively, you can encourage students to create trees and bushes made from cardboard, paper, wool etc. or even act them out on stage (it could simply be children holding word cards 'bush', 'tree' etc.)

Variations

1) Students add their own ideas to the script, e.g. by using adverbs of frequency (*Does he **always** do what you tell him? Does he **sometimes** break things?*).

2) Students change the script to fit a different theme, e.g. The perfect teacher/ the perfect friend/the perfect mum (dad). Encourage them to think of alternative ideas for endings that would work for those ideas (e.g. the perfect teacher is a puppet/teddy bear – hence never gives homework, never gets angry, never tells students to work harder etc.).

3) If you decide to share the role of 'Person 2' among several actors, then the students could decide to set the play somewhere else. Four people playing golf, for instance, would provide interesting and possibly amusing options physically. Whilst one character speaks, another attempts a lusty 'drive' or a tricky 'putt' with varying degrees of success.

Short sketches

Materials
Track 01

Photocopiable Worksheet p 185

- Comprehension check
- Vocabulary: words to describe people
- Present simple, third person singular

Short sketches

The Perfect Son

Track 01

Roles Person 1
Person 2

Scene Two people sitting on a park bench

PERSON 1   I have the perfect son.
PERSON 2   The perfect son? Nobody's perfect!
PERSON 1   My son is.
PERSON 2   Really? Does he never tell a lie?
PERSON 1   No, he doesn't.
PERSON 2   Does he never forget to do his homework?
PERSON 1   No, he doesn't. Never!
PERSON 2   Does he never use bad language?
PERSON 1   No, he doesn't.
PERSON 2   Does he never get bad marks at school?
PERSON 1   No, he doesn't.
PERSON 2   Does he never come home late?
PERSON 1   No, he doesn't.
PERSON 2   Is it true?
PERSON 1   Is what true?
PERSON 2   About your son. He doesn't tell lies, he never forgets to do his homework, he doesn't use bad language, he doesn't get bad marks at school. And he doesn't come home late. Is that all true?
PERSON 1   It is, believe me.
PERSON 2   Then you're right.
PERSON 1   Right? With what?
PERSON 2   He's the perfect son.
PERSON 1   I told you. He's the perfect son.
PERSON 2   You have the perfect son.
PERSON 1   Yeah, that's right.
PERSON 2   The perfect, perfect son.
PERSON 1   The perfect, perfect son!
PERSON 2   Fantastic! What's his name?
PERSON 1   Whose name?
PERSON 2   Your son's.
PERSON 1   Oh, my son's. Jonathan.
PERSON 2   He's great!

Person 1	Who's great?
Person 2	Your son.
Person 1	My son? Why's he so great?
Person 2	He doesn't tell lies, he never forgets to do his homework, he doesn't use bad language, he doesn't get bad marks at school. And he doesn't come home late.
Person 1	That's right.
Person 2	How old is he?
Person 1	How old's who?
Person 2	Your son.
Person 1	Oh, my son. He's eight.
Person 2	He's EIGHT?
Person 1	Yes – eight months!

Short sketches

2 Smart Shoppers

A sketch in 2 scenes

Track 02

Roles	3
Runtime	Around 2 minutes, depending on production
Sets	A living room; a clothes shop
Props	A dress, a coat, a blue scarf, a green scarf
Style	A parody on shoppers' arrogance and silly consumerism
Synopsis	A man and his wife go shopping for clothes. Through their insensitive and ridiculous behaviour they make fools of themselves.
Language level	Elementary – A2
Language areas	Language for shopping; admiring someone's clothes; making suggestions; telling someone what to do; showing annoyance; words for clothes
Stage tips	The sketch opens in the main characters' living room. A table, a few chairs, some pictures or posters on the wall, etc. can easily create the right atmosphere.
	The second part is set in a clothes shop. A few items of clothing and – if available – a table can be used to form the scenery.
Variations	If you want to practise other language areas with your students, the characters can buy other clothes or go to a different shop altogether. Because the sketch is very short it could also be used for improvisation – students read the text (or part of it), get a few minutes' preparation time, and then act out an improvisation, possibly with their own ending.
	Likewise, students can be asked to act out a continuation of the scene. A possible scenario could be for the couple to come back the next day. They are sorry for their behaviour on the previous day – but this time, the shop assistant surprises them …
Materials	Track 02

Photocopiable Worksheet p 186

- Comprehension check
- Vocabulary: clothes and shopping
- Making suggestions, telling someone what to do

Puchta/Gerngross/Devitt | Get on Stage! | © Helbling Languages

Short sketches

Smart Shoppers

Roles   Man
            Woman
            Shopkeeper

Scene 1 A living room. A man is sitting in a chair with his hands over his eyes.

MAN	Hurry up, darling.
WOMAN	(*off*) Just a minute, almost there.
MAN	I can't wait much longer. I'm so excited!
WOMAN	I'm coming right now, but no peeping!
MAN	I promise.
WOMAN	(*entering*) OK. You can look now.
MAN	(*taking his hands away*) At last!
WOMAN	(*twirling around*) Well? How do I look in my new dress?
MAN	You look marvellous, darling. Happy anniversary.
WOMAN	You're sure it doesn't make my bottom look a bit fat?
MAN	Not at all. But …
WOMAN	(*alarmed*) What? What's the matter? I look awful, don't I?
MAN	Calm down, darling – there's nothing wrong! It's just that you look so lovely in that dress I want to get you something else to match.
WOMAN	Oh my sweetie diddums dumpling! A scarf perhaps?
MAN	Yes, or a gorgeous coat.
WOMAN	Super! Let's go shopping!

Scene 2 A clothes shop

WOMAN	Look at the wonderful scarves.
MAN	Try on the blue one.
SHOPKEEPER	Can I help you?
WOMAN	No thanks. We're just looking.
MAN	The blue scarf is beautiful! … But it doesn't go with your dress.
WOMAN	(*to shopkeeper*) Hand me the green one.
SHOPKEEPER	Here you are. (*he hands her the green one, she gives him the blue one*)
WOMAN	Well?
SHOPKEEPER	It looks fantastic with your wonderful dress.
WOMAN	Thank you.
MAN	Darling, give it back and try that coat.
WOMAN	(*to shopkeeper*) Would you mind?

Short sketches

Shopkeeper	Of course not, madam. (*he takes the green scarf and hands her the coat*)
Woman	It's nice. I really like it.
Man	Good. We'll take it. Goodbye.
Shopkeeper	Where are you going? You haven't paid for the coat.
Man	She gave the green scarf back.
Woman	And the blue scarf.
Man	We exchanged the coat for the scarves.
Shopkeeper	But you didn't pay for the green scarf or the blue scarf either.
Man	Of course not. Why should I pay for something that I didn't buy?
Shopkeeper	But … but …
Woman	Let's go. Shopkeepers can be so unfriendly these days!

3 A Fast-Food Stall

A sketch in 1 scene

Track 03

Roles	7
Runtime	Around 5 minutes, depending on production
Set	A fast-food stall
Props	A table as the counter; if possible napkins of different colours; knives, forks and plates optional: various foods (hot dog, hamburger, fish & chips, onions, ketchup and mustard)
Style	A short, simple comedy sketch
Synopsis	How trying to get something to eat quickly at a fast-food stall turns out to be a painful experience for three customers – and a delight for three others!
Language level	Elementary – A2
Language areas	Ordering food at a fast-food place; polite requests; how polite requests can change when people are in a hurry

Vocabulary: fast food |
| **Stage tips** | Make sure your students differentiate clearly between the urgency expressed by the first three customers and the way the polite but slow assistant serves them. A good way of helping students to be able to do this well on stage (in an almost exaggerated manner) is to write a sentence on the board (e.g. Can I have a hamburger, please?) and prepare prompt cards with words on them (e.g. angry, tired, polite, unfriendly, nervous etc.). Tell students that they should say the sentence (in chorus, or alternatively individually when you point at students) as suggested by the prompt you are holding up each time.

Encourage your students to come up with different character types for the customer roles. They're all in a hurry but one might be a football fan, one a woman (or a man!) with a pushchair and one a very smart city high-flier. |
| **Variations** | Once students are well familiar with the language used, you can do an improvisation activity. Students act out a part of the sketch, but change the emotional disposition of one or several of the characters in the sketch, (e.g. the customers are extremely friendly, and the assistant is impatient, or even hungry). |

Short sketches

Materials

Photocopiable Worksheet p 187
- Comprehension check
- Vocabulary: ordering food and drinks
- Polite requests

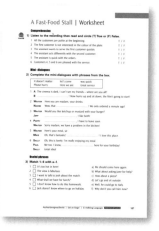

Short sketches

A Fast-Food Stall

Roles Assistant
Customers 1–6

Enter Customer 1.

Customer 1	A hamburger, please.
Assistant	Right. A hamburger.
Customer 1	Hurry up, please. I'm hungry.
Assistant	Ketchup?
Customer 1	Yes.
Assistant	Onions?
Customer 1	No.
Assistant	No onions?
Customer 1	No, please hurry up. I'm hungry.
Assistant	On a blue plate or a pink one?
Customer 1	Doesn't matter. *Hurry up!*

The shop assistant slowly presents various napkins.

Assistant	A red napkin?
Customer	Doesn't matter. Hurry up!
Assistant	A green napkin?
Customer 1	OK, a green napkin. *Please hurry!*

Enter Customer 2. The assistant slowly turns to the second customer.

Customer 2	A hot dog, please.
Assistant	Right. A hamburger.
Customer 2	No, not a hamburger. A hot dog.
Assistant	OK, a hot dog. Mustard?
Customer	Yes.
Assistant	Ketchup?
Customer	No.
Assistant	No ketchup?
Customer	No, hurry up. I'm hungry.
Assistant	On a blue plate or a pink one?
Customer	Doesn't matter. *Hurry up!*

The assistant presents various napkins.

Assistant	A red napkin?

Short sketches

CUSTOMER 2 Doesn't matter. Hurry up!

ASSISTANT A green napkin?

CUSTOMER 2 OK, a green napkin. *Please hurry!*

Enter Customer 3.

CUSTOMER 3 Fish and chips, please.

ASSISTANT Right. A hot dog.

CUSTOMER 3 No, I said fish and chips.

ASSISTANT Vinegar?

CUSTOMER 3 Yes.

ASSISTANT Ketchup?

CUSTOMER 3 No.

ASSISTANT No ketchup?

CUSTOMER 3 No! Hurry up, please. I'm hungry.

ASSISTANT On a blue plate or a yellow one?

CUSTOMER 3 Doesn't matter. *Hurry up!*

The assistant slowly presents various napkins.

ASSISTANT A red napkin?

CUSTOMER 3 Doesn't matter. Hurry up!

ASSISTANT A green napkin?

CUSTOMER 3 OK, a green napkin. *Please hurry!*

ASSISTANT OK, a hamburger with ketchup on a pink plate and a green napkin, a hot dog with mustard on a blue plate and a green napkin and fish and chips with vinegar on a yellow plate and a green napkin.

Assistant turns round to prepare the food. The three customers hear him singing to some rock music. They get more and more impatient, and after half a minute they leave, shouting 'I can't believe it!', 'Slow as a snail!', 'Terrible service!' and swearing. The audience can hear loud rock music. Meanwhile Customers 4, 5 and 6 appear. They listen to the music for a while, then they shout:

CUSTOMER 4 A hot dog, please.

CUSTOMER 5 A hamburger please.

CUSTOMER 6 Fish and chips, please.

Assistant appears with the food after 5 seconds.

ASSISTANT Where are they?

CUSTOMERS 4, 5, 6 Here we are.

ASSISTANT Ah! A hot dog, a hamburger and fish and chips.

Customers take the food and start eating.

Customer 4 That was quick. Wonderful!

Customer 5 Great service. Perfect!

Customer 6 Let's come here again tomorrow. I've never been served so fast!

Short sketches

4 Colin the Poet

A sketch in 1 scene

Track 04

Roles	6
Runtime	Around 5 minutes, depending on production
Set	At a breakfast table
Props	A table and 5 chairs, a letter, doorbell ringer device
Optional: items to go on table for breakfast (plates, cutlery, food etc.), a postbag
Style	A sketch (partly in the form of a rhyming comedy)
Synopsis	Colin's family find his love of rhyme very annoying, but things change when it turns out that he is the winner of a poetry competition.
Language level	Elementary – A2
Language areas	Offering food at a breakfast table; how to politely accept and refuse offers;

Vocabulary: breakfast

Phonology: rhyming pairs |
| **Stage tips** | This sketch thrives on the clash between Colin's love of rhyme and his family's initial annoyance about it. This should be well expressed through mime and gestures: when Colin creates his rhymes, he should be smiling, fully enjoying the sounds of his wordcraft, while the members of his family look more and more distressed and bored. This is in sharp contrast to the end of the scene. When it turns out that Colin has won a poetry competition and can choose one of his family to accompany him to New York, they should all smile at him in appreciation, and come across as enthusiastic and eager.

Be careful when staging a play set around a table that the audience can see all of the actors. In this case we suggest having two characters sat on one side of the table facing the audience and another two at each end of the table but with their chairs 'cheated' out on a slight angle towards the audience (if Mr or Mrs Atkins is reading the newspaper then they would naturally turn away from the table).

By the end of the play there are five characters on stage but instead of having all of them sitting down, either Mr or Mrs Atkins can be standing and fetching and carrying Colin's breakfast. Another table just behind the main table could be the worktop/cupboard. |
| **Variations** | Students can be asked to create different rhymes for the same bit of dialogue, or they can think of a different context altogether, e.g. Colin is with his classmates, |

Short sketches

during a break; they are talking about music, free time, their hobbies etc. and are getting increasingly annoyed with Colin, who can't stop creating rhymes. Finally, a teacher comes in with the great news …

To help students with creating rhymes it may be a good idea to encourage them to use a rhyming dictionary (several can be found online).

Materials
Track 04

Photocopiable Worksheet p 188
- Comprehension check
- Vocabulary: breakfast food
- Accepting and refusing offers

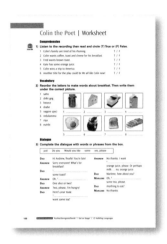

Short sketches

Colin the Poet

Roles Mr Atkins
Mrs Atkins
Colin, their son
Fred, his elder brother
Kate, his elder sister
Postie (*i.e. postman/woman*)

Scene Mr and Mrs Atkins are having breakfast. Enter Colin.

MR ATKINS Good morning, Colin.

COLIN Good morning, Dad,
Good morning, Mum –
It's Colin here,
Your poet son.

MR ATKINS Oh, Colin! (*rolling his eyes in desperation*) Tea?

COLIN One, two, three,
Tea for me.

MR ATKINS Stop it, Colin! Here's your tea.

MRS ATKINS Some toast?

COLIN Give me butter, give me bread,
My empty tummy must be fed.

MRS ATKINS Stop it, Colin. Please!

COLIN 'Stop it, Colin – Colin, please!'
My mother begs upon her knees.

MR AND MRS ATKINS Pleeease, Colin, pleeeeeease!

COLIN Please, please, oh please –
Give me some cheese.

Enter Fred.

FRED Morning, everybody.

MR AND MRS ATKINS Morning, Fred.

COLIN Good morning, Fred.
How was your bed?
I heard you roar –
Or did you snore?

FRED I don't snore!

COLIN Are you sure you do not snore?
It must have been a creaky door!

MRS ATKINS Would you like some toast with your tea?

Short sketches

FRED	Yes, please.
COLIN	D'you want your toast As white as a ghost?
FRED	Be *quiet*, Colin! I want brown crispy toast, please.
MRS ATKINS	Just a moment …
COLIN	'Just a moment,' says our mum; Two slices shall be made – Would you like some jam with those? Or p'rhaps some marmalade?
FRED	Colin, stop annoying us.

Enter Kate.

KATE	Morning, everybody.
MR AND MRS ATKINS/FRED	Morning
COLIN	Good morning, Kate! You're running late.
MR ATKINS	Orange juice?
KATE	No thanks. Can I have some tea?
MR ATKINS	Of course. And what would you like to eat?
KATE	Oh, just some toast, please. And can I have an egg?
MR ATKINS	Certainly.
COLIN	For lovely Kate Some toast on a plate – But let her beg For her nice fried egg.
KATE	Stop bugging me, Colin!
MR ATKINS	Colin, *please!* We want peace and quiet.
COLIN	In our house it's always quiet – We've never, ever had a riot. In our house there's always peace – There is no need for the police.
MR ATKINS	We'll *call* the police if you don't stop.

Doorbell rings.

MRS ATKINS	Can you open the door, Colin?
COLIN	(*going to open the door*) Certainly, Mum. That could be fun.
POSTIE	Good morning.

Short sketches

COLIN   There's nothing to fear –
The postie's here!

POSTIE   Are you Colin Atkins?

FRED   Yes, it's him, the crazy boy.

POSTIE   You've won the poetry competition. The prize is a trip to New York for two!

COLIN   A trip to New York
A trip for two –
Who shall I take …
Who, who, oh who?

All the members of the family get up and crowd around Colin, shouting to be the second person on the trip to New York.

ALL   Take me with you, Colin! Please, Colin, please! Let me go with you to New York! (etc.)

Short sketches

5 The Ticket

A sketch in 1 scene

Roles	3
Runtime	Around 3 minutes, depending on production
Set	In the street
Props	4 chairs to make a car Optional: a police officer's helmet/hat, a pair of handcuffs
Style	A short comedy sketch
Synopsis	A police officer stops a woman for jumping a red light. When the officer gives her a ticket, she understands and feels sorry for what she has done. Not so her husband. He behaves rather arrogantly – a bit too arrogantly!
Language level	Intermediate – B1
Language areas	Gerund after certain expressions (*I'm sorry for jumping the red light; I'm arresting you for insulting a police officer*); Conditional 2 (*Would I get a ticket if I called you …?*)
Stage tips	Ask the students to listen to the recording of the short sketch several times with their eyes closed. Ask them what they imagined while listening, e.g. how many people there were, what the situation was like, what the people were doing, how the people were feeling etc. Return to this activity later when the students are rehearsing the sketch. Play short scenes and ask the students to listen with their eyes closed. Get them to listen several times and to imitate as closely as possible the way the speaker on the audio says their lines.
Materials	 **Photocopiable Worksheet p 189** • Comprehension check • Gerunds • Vocabulary: apologising

Puchta/Gerngross/Devitt | Get on Stage! | © Helbling Languages

Short sketches

The Ticket

Roles Man
Woman
Police officer

Scene Woman and Man are sitting in a car (made of four chairs); Woman is at the steering wheel. They have been stopped by Police officer.

OFFICER Good evening, madam. Good evening, sir.
WOMAN Good evening, officer.
MAN (*grumpily*) I don't think this is a good evening at all.
OFFICER Madam, may I see your driving licence?
WOMAN Of course! But why?
OFFICER You jumped a red light.
WOMAN Did I really?
MAN (*to police officer*) She didn't!
OFFICER Sir, I'm not talking to you. I'm talking to this lady here.
MAN That's ridiculous!
OFFICER I'm warning you, sir.
WOMAN Please be quiet, Paul.
OFFICER You're right, madam. Thank you.
MAN How silly. But, we were not …
WOMAN Oh, Paul, please!
OFFICER (*giving woman a ticket*) Madam, I'm giving you a ticket.
WOMAN I understand. I'm sorry for jumping the lights.
MAN That's ridiculous.
OFFICER Sir, please calm down.
MAN Can I ask you a question?
OFFICER Of course.
MAN Would I also get a ticket if I called you an idiot?
OFFICER Yes, you would.
MAN What if I just thought that you were an idiot?
OFFICER I can't give you a ticket for what you think.
MAN Great. I think you're an idiot.
OFFICER Oh do you?
MAN Yes and *I think* you've got big ears and a pointy nose.

OFFICER	I see. Well, in that case *I think* you had better get out of the car.
MAN	Get out of the car? Why on earth would I want to do that? Don't you *think* I've got better things to do?
OFFICER	*I think* you probably have, sir, and *I know* you'll have plenty of time to *think* about them while you're in prison.
MAN	In prison!?
OFFICER	Yes sir; I'm arresting you for insulting a police officer.
MAN	But you said you couldn't arrest me for thinking.
OFFICER	I'm not arresting you for thinking – I'm arresting you for saying what you think.
MAN	What?!
OFFICER	(*putting on the cuffs*) I wonder if you can guess what I'm thinking now, sir?
WOMAN	Allow me, officer. He thinks you're an idiot, Paul.
OFFICER	Thank you, Madam. (*to audience*) It's always nice when people help the police with their work.

Short sketches

6 Being Polite

A sketch in 1 scene

Roles	6
Runtime	Around 6 minutes, depending on production
Set	A shop
Props	Table(s) for counter
Style	A sketch with minimal stage requirements, and a single set
Synopsis	An entertaining short play that shows that being impolite doesn't pay.
Language level	Intermediate – B1
Language areas	Going shopping; expressing politeness
Stage tips	To help students to fully identify with the mood swings of the customers (from being abrupt and impolite to showing states of growing politeness), it may be a good idea to do with the students a variation of the game described on p 43 in the Stage Tips section.

Draw the following graph on the board:

Explain to them that 0 on the scale is neutral, 3 is very polite, and -3 is very impolite. Get them to mime facial expressions for 0, 3 and -3. Then ask them to mime 0, 1, 2, 3, and finally -1, -2, and -3.

Dictate the following sentences, reading them to express the following degrees of politeness (as indicated in brackets), and ask the students to write down the number they think the sentence would take on the scale.
Could you possibly get me a hammer, please. (*very polite: 3*)
Get me a hammer right now. (*very impolite: -3*)
I'd like a hammer. (*neutral: 0*)
Good morning. I'd like a hammer, please. (*more polite: 2*)
Get me a hammer. (*more impolite: -2*)
Would you mind getting me a hammer? (*polite: 1*)
Where are your hammers? (*impolite: -1*)

Finally, write a different sentence on the board, expressing a neutral tone, e.g. *I want a screwdriver*. Get students to make this sentence more polite and more impolite. Show them how not only the words we use, but also body language, our facial expression and the stress and intonation influence whether a sentence we say comes across as polite or impolite.

Materials

Photocopiable Worksheet p 190

- Comprehension check
- Being polite or impolite
- Vocabulary: In a shop

Short sketches

Being Polite

Roles Shopkeeper
Shop assistant 1
Shop assistant 2
Customer 1
Customer 2
Customer 3

SHOPKEEPER	Good morning, sir. Welcome to our shop. Isn't it a lovely day?
CUSTOMER 1	Lovely day? I haven't got time for all that nonsense. Get me a hammer.
SHOPKEEPER	Sorry?
CUSTOMER 1	Get me a hammer, quickly!
SHOPKEEPER	Sorry?
CUSTOMER 1	What's the matter with you? Did you forget to clean your ears this morning? I said 'Get me a hammer! Right now.'
SHOPKEEPER	I heard you sir, but I think you forgot to say the magic word.
CUSTOMER 1	Magic word? What on earth are you talking about?
SHOP ASSISTANT 1	He heard you the first time, sir, but I think you are forgetting the magic word.
CUSTOMER 1	Magic word? You're as mad as him. I don't need a magic word, I need a hammer.
SHOP ASSISTANT 1	We know you need a hammer, sir. You've told us many times, but what we need is to hear the magic word.
CUSTOMER 1	The magic word? Magic word? What is this magic word?
SHOPKEEPER	The magic word
SHOP ASSISTANT 1	is
SHOP ASSISTANT 2	'please'!
CUSTOMER 1	Are you out of your mind? Do you know who I am? I am a very important person. I don't need to say please.
SHOPKEEPER AND HIS ASSISTANTS	Oh, sir. Everyone needs to say please.
CUSTOMER 1	And what if I don't?
SHOPKEEPER	If you don't
SHOP ASSISTANT 1	then we won't
SHOP ASSISTANT 2	let you have
SHOPKEEPER AND HIS ASSISTANTS	anything!
CUSTOMER 1	I see. Alright then. Get me a hammer p – p – p –
SHOPKEEPER	Go on, sir!
CUSTOMER 1	p – p – p –
SHOP ASSISTANT 1	You can do it!

Short sketches

Customer 1	p – p – p – please.
Shopkeeper and his assistants	Well done, sir.
Customer 1	You bunch of potato brains.
Shopkeeper and his assistants	Oh, dear sir.
Shopkeeper	Oh, dear me. I don't think you've understood.
Customer 1	What do you mean? I said 'please', didn't I?
Shop assistant 1	Yes, you did, but you didn't say it nicely.
Customer 1	What do you mean?
Shop assistant 2	You have to say it with a smile!
Shopkeeper	Watch. We'll show you.
Shopkeeper	Good day, madam. Can I help you? (*They are now talking to each other to give the customer an example*)
Shop assistant 1	Good day, I'd like a hammer please. (*smiling*)
Customer 1	Oh, I see.
Shop assistant 2	You understand?
Customer 1	Yes, I understand. Let me try.
Shopkeeper and his assistants	Certainly, sir.
Customer 1	I'd like a hammer, please. (*smiling*)
Shopkeeper	Well done, sir. You've got it.
Customer 1	Thank you.
Shopkeeper and his assistants	Our pleasure.
Shop assistant 2	That wasn't so bad, was it?
Customer 1	No, I must say, it feels good to be polite.
Shopkeeper	Well done, sir. (*he and assistants applaud*)
Customer 1	Thank you, thank you.

(*A second customer enters the shop.*)

Customer 2	Hey, you. Get me a screwdriver.
Customer 1	Sorry?
Customer 2	I wasn't talking to you. I was talking to them.
Customer 1	Sorry?
Customer 2	Mind your own business, potato brain. I've already told you I was talking to them and not to you!
Customer 1	They won't listen unless you say the magic word.

Short sketches

Customer 2	Magic word? What on earth are you talking about? I've had enough of this. You (*pointing at customer 1*) be quiet, and you (*pointing at shop assistants*) get me a screwdriver. I won't tell you again.
Shop assistant 1	You don't need to tell us again. We heard you the first time, madam.
Customer 1	What they didn't hear was the magic word.
Customer 2	Magic word? Magic word? What is this magic word?
Shopkeeper	The magic word
Assistants 1 and 2	is
Customer 1 and Assistants 1 and 2	'please'!
Customer 2	OK. Get me a screwdriver, please.
Customer 1	Now with a smile.
Customer 2	OK. Get me a screwdriver, please. (*smiles*)
Assistants 1 and 2	That was very nice, wasn't it?
Customer 1	Yes, it was. But …
Customer 2	But what?
Customer 1	I think you can be even nicer.
Customer 2	What could I say?
Customer 1	Well, repeat after me: Could you possibly get me a screwdriver, please?
Customer 2	Could you possibly get me a screwdriver, please?
Shopkeeper and his assistants	Wonderful.
Customer 2	Yeah, I must say, it feels good to be polite. But …
All	But what?
Customer 2	I think we can do even better than that, can't we?
Customer 1	Yes. I think we can.
Customers 1 and 2	Excuse us, dear shopkeepers.
Customer 1	Would you mind getting us a hammer
Customer 2	and a screwdriver,
Customers 1 and 2	please?
Shopkeeper and his assistants	That was fantastic.

(*A third customer enters the shop*)

Customer 3	Good day, one and all. I'm really sorry to interrupt your chat, but I would be really grateful if you could possibly get me a lovely saw.
Customer 2	Yes, and a screwdriver.
Customer 1	Yes, and a hammer.

Short sketches

All 3 customers	PLEASE!
Shopkeeper	We'd love to, dear customers
Shop assistant 1	but we're awfully sorry
Shop assistant 2	we have a small problem.
Customer 1	A problem?
Shop assistant 1	Yes, sir.
Customer 2	But we were really polite, weren't we?
Shop assistant 2	Yes, madam.
Customer 3	So why can't we have a hammer, a screwdriver and a saw?
Shopkeeper	Because, dear customers,
Shopkeeper and his Assistants	this is a shoe shop!

Short sketches

7 Parrot Learns a Lesson

A sketch in 4 scenes

Roles	Min 5 to max 8 (if roles are doubled)
Runtime	Around 5 minutes, depending on production
Set	John's place
Props	A headband with a few coloured feathers for the actor playing the parrot optional: 2 big boxes to make a cupboard and a freezer
Style	A single set sketch with minimal stage requirements
Synopsis	John has superb manners, but his parrot hasn't; it loves using bad language. When the bird keeps misbehaving on various embarrassing occasions, John has to come up with various forms of punishment. One of them finally works …
Language level	Intermediate – B1
Language areas	Imperatives (affirmative and negative)
Stage tips	1) Give your students a chance to listen to the audio recording of this play several times. Ask them to look at the script while they are listening, and get them to use a single colour to underline each of John's lines in the following manner:

green – polite
red – angry
blue – neutral

Then ask your students to work in small groups. Name a colour, e.g. green. The students take turns in reading out to each other one sentence they have underlined in that colour. The reading should be in-role, to express the mood as underlined.

Later you could carry on in the same way with the parrot's lines, e.g.

yellow – cheeky
orange – apologetic
pink – cunning, pretending to be nice

2) You can easily extend the minimum number of roles by doubling the actors for John and the parrot in Scenes 2–4. In order to make this possible, John and the parrot should each wear something that can easily be transferred to the next actor when they double their role, e.g. a hat for John, and a headband with coloured feathers for the parrot. Have John and the parrot exit after each scene.

Short sketches

Then a student appears carrying a board announcing the next scene. When John and the parrot re-appear (played by a different student), the audience should easily recognise them by the piece of clothing/the feathers that have been passed on from their predecessor.

Variation Encourage students to work in groups and write additional scenes for the sketch where other people come to visit (e.g. John's son's teacher, the queen herself; a neighbour who wants to complain about the parrot's language etc.)

When the groups have finished writing their short scenes, they act them out. The class decides on one (or several) scene(s) that get(s) added to the play for performance.

Materials
Track 06

Photocopiable Worksheet p 191
- Comprehension check
- Vocabulary: mini-dialogues

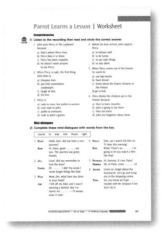

Short sketches

Parrot Learns a Lesson

Roles
John, the parrot's owner
Aunt Sophie
Uncle Henry
Lady Windermere
John's boss
John's boss's wife
Percy the parrot

Scene 1 John's home

JOHN (*to audience*) Hello everyone! My name's John. Do any of you have pets? I'm sure you do. And I'm sure they bring you great pleasure. Well, I have a pet, and here he is. This is my parrot, Percy. And Percy is a very clever animal. He can talk. That's good, isn't it? Unfortunately, when he speaks, he's often very rude. That's why I've asked him to really be good today. Because Uncle Henry and Auntie Sophie are coming to visit. They're very nice people, you see, and I wouldn't want to upset them.

Doorbell rings.

JOHN Ah, here they are. Remember, Percy – behave!

PARROT Percy good boy, good boy.

UNCLE HENRY Hi, John.

AUNT SOPHIE Hi, John. Good to see you.

JOHN Hi.

PARROT You monkey faces, get lost!

JOHN Percy! Stop that or I'll put you in the cupboard.

PARROT Oh, get lost, you idiots!

JOHN Percy! Into the cupboard with you. (*puts parrot into cupboard*)

PARROT Help, help! Call the police!

Scene 2 Two days later

JOHN (*to audience*) That was awful, wasn't it? But Percy must have learnt his lesson this time round. I certainly hope so, because tonight I'm expecting a visit from my boss and his wife. There's no way I'd want them to hear any rude words.

Doorbell rings.

JOHN Ah, here they are. Remember, Percy, behave!

PARROT Percy good boy, good boy!

JOHN'S BOSS Hi, John.

HIS WIFE Hi, John. Good to see you.

JOHN Hi, please come in.

PARROT Stinkers! Get lost!

JOHN Percy! Stop that or I'll put you in the wardrobe.

PARROT	Oh, get lost, you skunks!
JOHN	Percy! Into the wardrobe with you. (*puts parrot into wardrobe*)
PARROT	Help, help! Call the police!

Scene 3 **Two days later**

JOHN	(*to audience*) That was appalling, wasn't it? But I'm perfectly certain Percy's not going to misbehave next time. Tonight I'm expecting a visit from Lady Windermere. She's a friend of the queen, and if Percy uses any rude words I might get into serious trouble.

Doorbell rings.

JOHN	Ah, here she is. Remember, Percy, behave!
PARROT	Percy good boy, good boy.
LADY WINDERMERE	Hello John, my dear!
JOHN	Hello, Lady Windermere. Come right in.
PARROT	Get lost, you clonker!
JOHN	Percy! Stop that or I'll put you in the freezer.
PARROT	Oh, you dunderhead, get lost!
JOHN	(*putting parrot into freezer*) Into the freezer with you.

Scene 4 **Half an hour later**

JOHN	I think I'll have to take the parrot out.

Opens freezer and gets parrot out.

PARROT	I'm freezing!
JOHN	Then don't use bad words when you talk to my friends.
PARROT	All right, I promise. Never again, John!
JOHN	Good.
PARROT	But can I ask you a question?
JOHN	What is it, parrot?
PARROT	There are some frozen chickens in the freezer.
JOHN	So what?
PARROT	Well, you put them there, right?
JOHN	Of course I did.
PARROT	Then please tell me …
JOHN	Tell you what?
PARROT	Well, those poor chickens … what did *they* say?

Short sketches

8 Granddad's Birthday

A sketch in 2 scenes

Track 07

Roles	4 (up to 8 if roles are doubled)
Runtime	Around 5 minutes, depending on production
Sets	Mark, Lily and Emma's place; Granddad's place
Props	A walking stick for Granddad; a birthday cake (can be made of foam rubber decorated to look like a cake with squishy cream on top) optional: if roles get doubled, each of the actors should have something prominent that can easily be transferred to their successors (e.g. Mark, a certain cap; Lily, a T-shirt of some memorable design, Emma, a pair of colourful glasses, and for Granddad, the walking stick)
	If possible a few pieces of furniture (e.g. chairs and a table)
Style	A sketch with no specific stage requirements
Synopsis	It's Granddad's 90th birthday, and Mark, Lily and Emma each want to give him a very special present. Their presents are indeed unique, but what Granddad does with them is even more original!
Language level	Intermediate – B1
Language areas	Giving advice (*why don't you give him a …*); expressing intentions (*I'm going to give him a …*); asking if someone liked a present (*How did you like …? Did you like …?*); narrating (*I didn't like the colour, so I gave it to …*)
Stage tips	There are various options of indicating to the audience that there is a change of set when Scene 1 finishes. You can either have a student walk across the stage with a sign reading *Scene 2: Granddad's place*, or the actors change the set before they go off at the end of Scene 1 (by changing the position of the furniture). The change of set could be made clearer to the audience through a student walking across the stage showing a sign as suggested just above.
Variation	Creative classes could (with or without your help) add a few grandchildren and original ideas for presents and what Granddad does with them!

Short sketches

Materials

Photocopiable Worksheet p 192

- Comprehension check
- Giving advice
- Vocabulary: talking about what happened

Short sketches

Granddad's Birthday

Roles Granddad
Mark
Lily
Emma

Scene 1 **Mark, Lily and Emma's home**

MARK It's Granddad's 90th birthday next week. I don't know what to give him. He's so difficult to please. Have you thought about a present?

LILY Well, I know that he's difficult to please, but …

EMMA But what?

LILY I'm going to give him a …

EMMA Come on, Lily.

LILY A shiny black Rolls Royce.

MARK A Rolls? I can't believe it. Granddad doesn't drive any more. You didn't forget that, did you?

LILY No, I didn't. Granddad is very difficult to please, so the black Rolls comes with …

MARK With what? Come on Lily!

LILY A driver.

EMMA Oh, that's a brilliant idea. It will make him very happy.

MARK Great. What can I give him?

LILY Why don't you give him a painting? He likes paintings.

MARK Brilliant idea. I'm going to give him a Sandarello.

EMMA A Sandarello?

MARK He's a famous painter from the States. I saw a painting yesterday at Johnson's, the art dealer. It's an abstract painting called *Sunset 87* and it costs £120,000.

LILY I'm sure Granddad will like that. What about your present, Emma?

EMMA I'm going to give him a parrot.

LILY A parrot? What for?

EMMA It's a very special parrot. It can speak.

MARK It can really speak?

EMMA Yes, it can. You know that Granddad loves poems. The parrot knows loads of them. He can say them all by heart.

MARK Great present!

LILY Yes, I'm sure Granddad will like it a lot.

EMMA He'll love it. Hey, why don't we visit Granddad the weekend after his birthday? We can bake him a cake and he can thank us for the presents.

MARK Fantastic idea! Can't wait to see his smiley old face.

Short sketches

LILY	Just hope he remembers to put his teeth in!
EMMA	(*a bit perplexed*) OK! See you next weekend.
MARK	See you!

They exit from one side of the stage and then Granddad enters from the other side with a walking stick, walking very slowly in a comedy 'old folks silly walk' style.

Scene 2 Granddad's place

Enter Lily, Emma and Mark. Emma is holding a cake.

LILY/MARK/EMMA	Good afternoon, Granddad.
GRANDDAD	Ah, Lily, Mark and Emma.
ALL THREE	How are you, Granddad?
GRANDDAD	I'm fine.
LILY	Granddad?
GRANDDAD	Yes, Lily?
LILY	How did you like the presents?
GRANDDAD	Presents?
EMMA	For your birthday.
GRANDDAD	Ah, those.
LILY	How did you like the Rolls?
GRANDDAD	I didn't like its colour. How could you give me a black car? Black is for old people. I gave it away.
LILY	You gave it away …
GRANDDAD	Yes, to my gardener's son. He's just turned 18. Every morning he picks up his favourite teacher and drives her to school.
LILY	What about the driver?
GRANDDAD	I fired him.
LILY	Oh, no! (*falls unconscious on chair nearby*)
MARK	How do you like my picture, *Sunset 87*?
GRANDDAD	I got dizzy when I looked at it. So I gave it to the housemaid.
MARK	Does she like it?
GRANDDAD	No, she sold it.
MARK	I can't believe it. She sold it?
GRANDDAD	Yes, at the flea market.
MARK	Not really.
GRANDDAD	Yes, she was lucky. Some idiot paid £50 for it.

Short sketches

MARK Oh, no! (*falls unconscious on chair nearby*)

EMMA I hope you liked my present, Granddad.

GRANDDAD Oh, Emma, my darling! Of course I did. You know what your granddad loves, don't you!

EMMA Well, I hope so.

GRANDDAD Well, it was excellent.

EMMA It was? I hope you didn't give it to the gardener's son.

GRANDDAD No, why? I wanted it for myself.

EMMA Oh, really? Thanks, Granddad.

GRANDDAD I gave it to the cook, my darling.

EMMA To the cook? To sell it at the flea market like the housemaid did?

GRANDDAD Oh, no, no, no, no, no! I simply gave it to the cook.

EMMA To the cook? What for?

GRANDDAD What for? What for? Don't be silly. It was delicious.

EMMA It was delicious? What was?

GRANDDAD The chicken. It was the best chicken I've ever had!

EMMA Oh no! That wasn't a chicken. It was a very expensive talking parrot!

GRANDDAD A talking parrot?

EMMA Yes, a talking parrot!

GRANDDAD Then why didn't it call for help?

EMMA Ohh!

She faints and her face falls into the cake, covering her face in cream.

Short sketches

The Princess and the Ring

 A modern fairy tale in 2 scenes
Track 08

Note	In this play, an otter who helps a princess to get her golden ring back asks her to kiss him. The actors pretend that they are kissing each other by going behind a bush and making kissing sounds. If you have selected this play to be acted out by your students, and you feel that such a scene is culturally unacceptable in the context in which you teach, you may want to change the scene. For example, the otter could say, 'Give me a little tickle behind my ears'. This is less overt and less fun, but it's still something that a Princess might not wish to be seen doing in public. A kiss is better, though!
Roles	5
Runtime	Around 5 minutes, depending on production
Sets	The castle garden; in the castle
Props	A crown (made of paper) for the king; a princess dress and a hat for Princess Rita (whereas Princess Flora is in jeans and T-shirt); a prince's clothes and a crown for Prince Humphrey; an otter mask; a Beckham/Ronaldo mask; a big plastic bathtub or bowl to represent the pond; something to make a T-shirt dirty with; some 'pond weeds'; a bush made of cardboard
Style	A modern fairy tale; it could be put on stage without props, but your students and the audience will enjoy the play far better with the props listed.
	N.B.: Although this is a fairy tale, it is probably better to have this acted out by teenagers rather than young learners as the play draws on quite a bit of irony and exaggeration – teens will be better able to put this across on stage than young learners!
Synopsis	When Princess Flora's golden ring falls into the pond in the garden of the castle, she gets help neither from her smug sister nor from Humphrey, the prince who wants to marry her. Help comes when an otter appears, but he wants to be kissed in exchange for returning the ring …
Language level	Upper Intermediate – B2
Language areas	*Can/can't* for expressing ability (*I can't get it; it's too deep*) *can/can't* for expressing permission (*You're a princess. You can't run around in jeans and a T-shirt*); making and refusing offers (*You can have a pencil; No, thank you.*)
Stage tips	1) Before your students read the script, get them to listen to the audio once or twice. Ask some specific questions afterwards, e.g. • Who are the people in the play? • Where are they?

Puchta/Gerngross/Devitt | Get on Stage! | © Helbling Languages

Short sketches

- One of the two princesses has got a problem – what is it?
- How does she try to solve the problem?
- Who helps her?
- What is the ending of the story?
- What differences are there between the two princesses, and between the two princes?
- Which of the people is best described by the following adjectives?

    friendly – helpful – proud – silly – clever

    Give your reasons.

2) Use the adjectives above to 'lead' the students into their respective roles, e.g. if students say that Princess Rita is very proud, discuss with the group how this would be expressed in the way she speaks. Get them to listen to the audio again to check.

Materials

Track 08

Photocopiable Worksheet p 193

- Comprehension check
- Vocabulary: in the garden
- *Can/be allowed to*

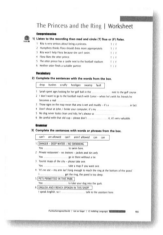

Short sketches

The Princess and the Ring

Roles Princess Flora   Princess Rita   Prince Humphrey   Otter/Prince Otto

Scene 1   In the garden of the castle

A football bounces onto the stage closely followed by a girl in jeans and a T-shirt.

Princess Flora	Beckham (Ronaldo/whoever) shoots, Beckham scores! (*she pretends to celebrate with the 'crowd' then gradually she saddens*) I'd love to be a footballer but I can't because I'm a princess, you see, and princesses aren't allowed to play football. In fact, princesses aren't allowed to do much at all other than marry princes. Being a princess is not something I'm very good at.
Princess Rita	(*calling, off*) Flora! Where are you?
Princess Flora	Oh dear. Here comes my sister, Princess Rita. She's a proper princess. She always gets 100% in princess exams and loves wearing diamonds.
Princess Rita	Ah! There you are, I've been looking everywhere. Well, I haven't, but my servants have. They told me you were here.
Princess Flora	What did you want me for?
Princess Rita	Handsome Prince Humphrey is here. He wants to see you.
Princess Flora	Me? Why?
Princess Rita	I've no idea why! I mean why would Handsome Prince Humphrey want to spend time with a scruffy girl like you? ... Unless ...
Princess Flora	Unless what?
Princess Rita	Unless he's fallen in love with ME, (*to audience*) easily done, you know, (*to Flora*) and he wants to ask you how to win my heart. He's probably terrified by my great beauty, poor thing.
Prince Humphrey	(*entering*) Stand aside! Handsome Prince approaching! Feel free to cheer! (*encourages audience to cheer*) Which one of you two lucky girls is Princess Flora?
Princess Flora	Me, why?
Prince Humphrey	My card. (*He hands her a business card*) Haven't got time to go into too much detail, due at the hairdresser's in 20 minutes, but basically my dad and your dad have arranged for us to be married.
Princess Rita	Her! Why her? Why not me? I'm a proper princess. She's a football hooligan.
Prince Humphrey	She's the eldest and, in the Government Guide to Fairy-tale Romances, it's the eldest daughter that gets to marry a handsome prince first. Bad luck, sweetie!
Princess Flora	Wait! I have something to say.
Prince Humphrey	I know! You probably want to tell me you're the luckiest girl alive but I know that already and in any case I haven't finished talking. Flora? ... You may answer.
Princess Flora	Yes? What is it?
Prince Humphrey	One little problem. You are a princess.

Puchta/Gerngross/Devitt | Get on Stage! | © Helbling Languages **PHOTOCOPIABLE**

Short sketches

Princess Flora Yes, I know.

Prince Humphrey And a princess can't run around in jeans and a T-shirt. I'm leaving now, but please try not to cry. When I return I want you dressed properly. I have an engagement ring for you here and I would put it on your finger but your hands are dirty so you'll have to put it on yourself.

Princess Flora (*ironically*) How romantic!

Prince Humphrey And now a kiss!

Princess Flora What?!!

Prince Humphrey (*to Princess Rita*) Do you have a mirror?

Princess Rita Yes, here. (*She hands him a small hand mirror*)

Prince Humphrey (*kisses his own reflection*). You handsome beast! (*to audience*) I'm leaving, feel free to swoon.

He exits.

Princess Rita Gosh. He really is handsome, isn't he? It's not fair. Why you?

Princess Flora It's not my fault!

Princess Rita Let me see the ring.

Princess Flora Look.

Princess Rita It's beautiful. Let me try it on.

Princess Flora No, sorry, I don't want to lose it. I may not want to marry him but a princess must do her duty.

Princess Rita Come on. I'm your sister. Trust me.

Princess Flora OK. But only for a minute.

Princess Flora takes the ring off and hands it to Rita.

Princess Rita It's nice. I like it.

Princess Flora Please give it back.

Princess Rita Here you are. Oops.

Rita drops the ring on purpose and it falls into a pond.

Princess Flora Look what you've done! You've dropped it in the pond!

Princess Rita I'm sorry. (*voice tells audience that she isn't*)

Princess Flora I can't get it, it's too deep. (*She lies in the grass and puts her hand into the water. She gets dirty and there are weeds on her arms.*)
Please, Rita, try to get it out.

Princess Rita Sorry, Flora, but my dress would get wet and dirty.

Short sketches

PRINCESS FLORA	I know! (*on her mobile, reading from the business card*) Humphrey, please come and help me. My new ring has fallen into the pond.
	She listens, then looks desperate.
PRINCESS RITA	What did he say?
PRINCESS FLORA	He won't come. He doesn't want to make his clothes dirty.
PRINCESS RITA	Oh dear, now you're in real trouble.
PRINCESS FLORA	So will you be when I tell Dad what you've done.
PRINCESS RITA	(*realising this is true*) Oh no! I didn't think of that.
	Both princesses start crying. Enter Otter.
OTTER	Why are you crying?
PRINCESS FLORA	She dropped my golden ring into the pond. (*she points at Rita*)
OTTER	Oh, dear!
PRINCESS FLORA	(*crying bitterly*) What can I do now?
OTTER	I've got an idea.
PRINCESS RITA	You? But you're an ugly otter.
PRINCESS FLORA	Let him speak.
OTTER	I may be ugly, but I can get it for you.
PRINCESS RITA	You mean … the ring?
OTTER	That's right. Give me a second.
	Otter dives into the pond and comes back with the ring. He is covered in weeds.
OTTER	Mmm. It looks wonderful.
PRINCESS RITA	Give it back to my sister. Quick.
OTTER	You dropped your sister's ring, didn't you?
PRINCESS RITA	Give it back, you ugly animal.
OTTER	OK, but what will you give me for it?
PRINCESS RITA	You can have a pencil.
OTTER	No, thank you. Hehehehehe.
PRINCESS RITA	You can have my handkerchief.
OTTER	Your handkerchief? No, thanks. Hehehehehe.
PRINCESS RITA	So what do you want?
OTTER	Give me a kiss.
PRINCESS RITA	No way. I would never kiss a wet and ugly otter.
PRINCESS FLORA	Rita, please kiss the otter.
PRINCESS RITA	No way.
PRINCESS FLORA	OK, then I'll do it. Let's go behind the bushes.

Short sketches

PRINCESS RITA Don't do it, sister!

Princess Flora and the Otter leave. We hear the sound of kissing. After a short time Princess Flora appears with a young man who is still a bit wet and covered with weeds and has a Beckham/Ronaldo mask on.

OTTER Here's the ring. (*handing it to Flora*)

PRINCESS RITA Who is that?

OTTER Well, it's a long story about a young prince and a magician's curse.

PRINCESS FLORA Come with us to the castle. I want you to meet my father!

PRINCESS RITA You can't invite this dirty young man.

PRINCESS FLORA Yes, I can.

Scene 2   In the castle

PRINCE HUMPHREY Make way! Your hero has returned. (*he spots Flora*) Flora, I can't believe it. After all I said! You are wet and there are weeds all over you. And you smell like a swamp. I can't marry a princess who can't behave herself.

PRINCESS FLORA You don't have to, Humphrey. Your clothes look nice, but I don't want to marry a prince who doesn't come when I need help. Here's your ring back. Goodbye.

PRINCE HUMPHREY Where are you going?

PRINCESS FLORA Well, this young man here wants to show me his castle.

PRINCE OTTO It's right next to the football stadium. I hope you don't mind.

PRINCESS FLORA My hero!

They leave together.

PRINCE HUMPHREY Boo hoo. I want my mummy.

PRINCESS RITA Don't cry, Humphrey. I'll marry you.

PRINCE HUMPHREY Have you brushed your teeth?

PRINCESS RITA Yes. Why?

PRINCE HUMPHREY Then you may kiss me.

She kisses him on the cheek.

PRINCESS RITA Have you washed your hands?

PRINCE HUMPHREY Of course! Why?

PRINCESS RITA Then you may hold my hand while we go and talk to Daddy.

They exit happily.

Short sketches

10 At the Doctor's

A comedy series of very short sketches, in 6 scenes

Roles	11
Runtime	Around 10 minutes, depending on production (but could be shortened by skipping one or several of the sketches)
Sets	Alternates between the doctor's surgery, the waiting room and the reception area. These could be 3 locations on the stage, next to one another:
	Surgery: a desk with a chair behind it for the doctor, on the wall an eyesight check chart (could easily be made by the students)
	Waiting room: a semi-circle of 5 chairs
	Reception area: a desk with a toy telephone and calendar on it, and a chair behind the desk for the receptionist
Props	White shirts for the doctor and the nurse (it's best to use men's shirts, worn back to front); big flip-over calendar with 5 pages, showing Monday 9, Tuesday 10, Wednesday 11, Thursday 12, Friday 13; for Patient 2, a paper bag with two eyeholes cut into it
	Optional: a toy stethoscope, a thermometer to check the body temperature; a walking stick for Patient 4 (old man); a biscuit as the 'pill' for Patient 5 to eat; red face paint or make-up for Patient 8's ears; a bucket
Style	A fast-paced series of very short sketches, all bound together within a single theme
Synopsis	It's a busy week for Dr Miller and Nurse Nancy. There are lots of patients, hardly any of them without an unusual problem. In spite of the doctor's creative treatments, things get more and more out of hand …
Language level	Upper Intermediate – B2
Language areas	The present perfect (*You've broken your finger*); past progressive vs. past simple (*I was ironing when the phone rang*); vocabulary: parts of the body; medical expressions (*a patient, a prescription, a hearing aid, do a test, take a pill, soak your swollen leg in the water; call the ambulance, feel well, make an appointment*) and phrases to describe symptoms (*a swollen leg, I can't hear well, my leg hurts, feel well*)
Stage tips	This is rather a long series of sketches, but there are not too many lines for each of the actors playing the patients. The roles of the doctor and the nurse, however, are more demanding. If necessary, they could be doubled. If the doctor for example has a white coat and the nurse a nurse's hat then they could be swapped between the actors and the characters would still remain easily identifiable (see p 62 for suggestions on how to do this best on stage to reduce the number of lines that the actors of these roles have to study).

Short sketches

Variation   The individual short sketches that this play consists of have been developed from jokes we found on the internet. You may want to do a project with your students where you look for suitable jokes on the web and get your students to turn them into a script for a play. If you want to do that, make sure you select jokes that are suitable for the age group you are teaching. Ask your students to work in groups. Give each group a photocopy of one of the jokes and ask them to turn it into a short dialogue. This could be done before or after the students read this script. If students come up with dialogues that are well suited to being acted out, they could be added to the play (or acted out after the play). In this case, it would be well worth stressing to the audience that the scripts for the short sketches were writen by the students themselves.

Materials

Photocopiable Worksheet A p 194
- Comprehension check
- Medical expressions
- Vocabulary: parts of the body

Photocopiable Worksheet B p 195
- Mini dialogue
- Vocabulary: medical expressions
- Past progressive vs. simple past; present perfect

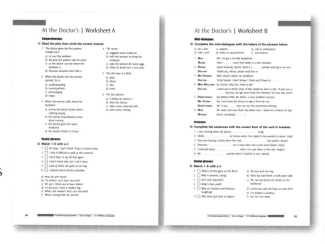

Short sketches

At the Doctor's

Roles   Dr Miller
Nurse Nancy
Receptionist
Patients 1–8 (Patient 3 is a woman, Patient 4 is an old man)

Scene 1   The Doctor's Waiting Room, Friday 13th

A receptionist sits at a desk. She has a little flip-over calendar on her desk that shows 'Friday 13th'.

RECEPTIONIST   They say that Friday the 13th is unlucky, don't they? Well, let me tell you this whole week has been mad!

NURSE   (*enters – to receptionist*) Good morning, Sally/Simon.

RECEPTIONIST   Morning, Nurse Nancy.

NURSE   (*looking at audience*) Looks like we've got a lot of sick patients this morning. Don't they look terrible?

RECEPTIONIST   Yes, especially that one. (*points at teacher*) I've just been telling them about our crazy week.

DOCTOR   Good morning, everyone.

RECEPTIONIST /NURSE   (*together*) Good morning, Dr Miller.

DOCTOR   What a week we've had.

RECEPTIONIST   Yes, Doctor. I was just explaining or do you want to?

DOCTOR   No! It will make me cry and anyway (*looks at audience*) it looks like Nurse Nancy and I are going to have a busy day. (*points to a member of the audience*) That one's yellow! Carry on.

Dr Miller and Nurse Nancy exit into doctor's surgery.

RECEPTIONIST   OK. (*she flips the calendar back to 'Monday 9th' as she says*) Well, it all began last Monday.

Scene 2   Monday 9th

PATIENT 1   (*storming into the reception area*) I need to see the doctor immediately.

RECEPTIONIST   I'm sorry, but the doctor is busy.

PATIENT 1   Please, please, I need to see the doctor.

RECEPTIONIST   What's the problem?

PATIENT 1   I've been bitten by a vampire.

RECEPTIONIST   Goodness gracious, I'll see what I can do.

Short sketches

Receptionist goes into surgery with patient. Dr Miller and Nurse Nancy are playing cards or doing something silly.

DOCTOR	Can't you see we're busy!
RECEPTIONIST	Sorry, Doctor, but this man here says he's been bitten by a vampire.
DOCTOR	Where did the vampire bite you?
PATIENT 1	Near the railway station.
NURSE	No, the doctor means where on your body?
PATIENT 1	Oh! Here, in the neck.
DOCTOR	Nurse, give him a glass of orange juice.
PATIENT 1	Orange juice? Why orange juice?
DOCTOR	Because it's yellow.
PATIENT 1	Yellow?
DOCTOR	Yes.
NURSE	Here you are.
DOCTOR	Drink up.
PATIENT 1	Will it make me better?
DOCTOR	No, I but can see if your neck leaks.
PATIENT 1	Ah, that's good.
DOCTOR	Nurse, plaster please. I can see the holes.

(Nurse handing over plaster, doctor putting plaster on patient's neck.)

DOCTOR	That should do it.
PATIENT 1	Thank you, Doctor.

(He/she leaves)

DOCTOR	Next patient, please, Nurse.
NURSE	(*calling into reception*) Next patient, please.
PATIENT 2	Good morning, Doctor.
DOCTOR	Good morning. What can I do for you?
PATIENT 2	When I looked in the mirror this morning, I was shocked.
DOCTOR	Why?
PATIENT 2	I saw an ugly man, with wrinkled skin and fuzzy hair.
DOCTOR	And?
PATIENT 2	And red eyes. And the colour of my skin ...
DOCTOR	Well?
PATIENT 2	It was white, like on a dead man. Doctor, what's wrong with me?

Doctor looks at the man for some time.

Short sketches

DOCTOR	Well, the only thing I can say is that there is nothing wrong with your eyesight.

Doctor and Nurse laugh uproariously. Patient looks sad.

DOCTOR	Sorry. I think we can give you something to help, can't we Nurse?
PATIENT 2	Really?
NURSE	Yes, really. Here you are. (*She puts a paper bag over the patient's head with two eyeholes cut in. Patient staggers off.*)

Scene 3   Tuesday 10th

RECEPTIONIST	(*turning the calendar to 'Tuesday 10th'*) So that was Monday and then on Tuesday …
DOCTOR	(*to nurse*) Call the next patient.
NURSE	What shall I call them? A rude name?
DOCTOR	No! Call them in here.
NURSE	Oh! (*calling into reception.*) Next please.
WOMAN (PATIENT 3)	Good morning, Doctor.
DOCTOR	Good morning. What can I do for you?
WOMAN	Well, it's about my husband.
DOCTOR	Your husband? Is he here?
WOMAN	No, he isn't.
DOCTOR	So, what's the problem?
WOMAN	Well, he thinks he's a chicken.
DOCTOR	How do you know?
WOMAN	Well, every morning he gets out of bed.
DOCTOR	He gets out of bed?
WOMAN	He does.
DOCTOR	Every morning?
WOMAN	Yes, he does.
DOCTOR	That's nothing unusual. Millions of people get out of their beds every morning.
WOMAN	I know.
DOCTOR	So?
WOMAN	Well, then he goes to the shed.
DOCTOR	That's nothing unusual. Millions of people …
WOMAN	Stop, Doctor! Please listen. He gets out of bed, he goes to the shed … and …
DOCTOR	And?
WOMAN	He cackles and makes a small nest.
DOCTOR	Mmh. How long has this been going on?

Short sketches

WOMAN	For a year, I think.
DOCTOR	For a year! A year?
WOMAN	Yes, a year!
DOCTOR	Why didn't you come earlier?
WOMAN	Well, I wanted to, but …
DOCTOR	But what?
WOMAN	Well, it was nice having a fresh egg from the shed every morning.
DOCTOR	That's great. Come again when your husband stops laying eggs.
WOMAN	Thank you, Doctor.
NURSE	We'll build him a nice nest.
DOCTOR	Nurse, please call in the next patient.
NURSE	Next please.
OLD MAN (PATIENT 4)	Good morning, Doctor.
DOCTOR	Good morning. What can I do for you?
OLD MAN	Eh?
DOCTOR	I said, what can I do for you?
OLD MAN	Sorry?
NURSE	(*bellowing*) What can we do for you?!
OLD MAN	Cock-a-doodle-do? I don't think I'm a chicken – that was the last one. I can't hear well.
DOCTOR	OK, let's do a test. Nurse, would you mind?

Nurse stands behind the patient and claps her hands.

DOCTOR	Did you hear that?
OLD MAN	(*silence*)
NURSE	(*bellowing*) Did you hear that?
OLD MAN	Have you done it yet?
DOCTOR	OK. I'll give you a prescription for a hearing aid. Go to the shop in Bond Street. They are the best. And come to see me tomorrow morning.

Scene 4   **Wednesday 11th**

RECEPTIONIST	(*turning the calendar to show 'Wednesday 11th'*) Sure enough, the next morning … Mr Brown to see you, Doctor.
OLD MAN	No need to shout, young lady/man.
RECEPTIONIST	(*whispers.*) Mr Brown to see you, Doctor.
DOCTOR	How's your hearing, Mr Brown?
OLD MAN	It's perfect.
DOCTOR	Let's do a test. Nurse?

Short sketches

Nurse stands behind the patient and claps her hands.

DOCTOR Did you hear that?

OLD MAN Of course. She was clapping her hands.

DOCTOR One more test.

Nurse stands behind the patient and clicks her fingers.

DOCTOR Did you hear that?

OLD MAN Of course. She was clicking her fingers.

DOCTOR And one final test.

Nurse mimes pricking her finger and dropping the pin.

OLD MAN Listen! I just heard a pin drop.

DOCTOR You and your family must be very happy that you can hear again.

OLD MAN Well, I haven't told them. I just sit around and listen when they're talking.

DOCTOR You haven't told them?

OLD MAN No, I just listen.

DOCTOR You just listen?

OLD MAN Yes and I have changed my will four times already.

DOCTOR And the next patient, please, Nurse.

NURSE Sorry, Doctor. I'm too tired after all that clapping and clicking. I need a sleep.

She lies down on the doctor's couch and falls asleep.

DOCTOR Next patient, please.

PATIENT 5 Good morning, Doctor.

DOCTOR Good morning. What can I do for you?

PATIENT 5 Please look at my leg. It hurts.

DOCTOR Mmm. It's badly swollen. Does this hurt? *(pinches the man's leg)*

PATIENT 5 Aaaaaaaaah.

DOCTOR Just a moment. *(rummaging in cupboard)* Here's a pill.

PATIENT 5 Wow. I've never seen such a big pill.

DOCTOR I'll be right back with some water. Try not to wake the nurse.

PATIENT 5 *(mumbling to him/herself)* Where is she? Ah, I can do it myself.

Patient goes to water fountain/wash basin, drinks and tries to swallow the big pill. He/She finally succeeds after a lot of struggling.

DOCTOR Here I am. And here's the water. *(He has put a bucket of water in front of the patient)*

PATIENT 5 What's the bucket for?

DOCTOR Well, you first put the pill in and then you soak your swollen leg in it for thirty minutes.

Short sketches

PATIENT 5 (*clutches his/her throat and faints*)

DOCTOR Nurse, wake up and call the ambulance!

Scene 5 **Thursday 12th**

RECEPTIONIST (*flipping the calendar to show 'Thursday 12th'.*) Thursday was no better, even though it was my birthday. (*to audience*) Go on, sing!

Doctor and Nurse lead audience as they sing 'Happy Birthday To You' (Maybe the Doctor indicates a medical chart where the words are miswritten:

Happy Birthday to You,

Happy Birthday to You.

You look like a monkey

And you smell like one, too.

OR

Happy Birthday to you

I went to the zoo

I saw a big monkey

And I thought it was you.)

NURSE Next patient, please.

PATIENT 6 Good morning, Doctor.

DOCTOR Good morning. What can I do for you?

PATIENT 6 I'm not feeling well, Doctor.

DOCTOR OK, let's have a look.

Takes his/her temperature and listens to his/her breathing, etc. Mutters to him/herself 'Mm' and 'Ahh'.

PATIENT 6 What's wrong with me, Doctor?

Doctor goes to cupboard, rummages around and comes back with three bottles of pills.

DOCTOR We'll explain. When you wake up, take a green pill with a big glass of water.

PATIENT 6 OK, I get it. A green pill in the morning with a big glass of water.

NURSE After lunch, take a red pill with a big glass of water.

PATIENT 6 OK, I get it. A red pill after lunch with a big glass of water.

DOCTOR Before you go to bed, take a blue pill with a big glass of water.

PATIENT 6 OK, I get it. Before I go to bed, I take a blue pill with a big glass of water. Can I ask you a question, Doctor?

DOCTOR Of course. Shoot.

PATIENT 6 So many different pills, Doctor, what exactly is my problem?

Short sketches

Doctor	You're not drinking enough water.
Nurse	Next patient please. (*She pushes the patient towards the door.*) Quickly!

The patients cross as one enters and one leaves.

Doctor	What's your problem?
Patient 7	Well, it hurts when I do this. (*He prods his chest with his finger.*) And, when I do this. (*He prods his leg with the same finger.*) And, when I do this. (*He prods his head with the same finger.*)
Nurse	I know what's wrong, Doctor.
Patient 7	What?
Nurse	You've broken your finger.
Doctor	Well done, Nurse!

Scene 6   Friday 13th

Receptionist	(*As she flips the calendar back to original 'Friday 13th'.*) And that brings us back to today. Let's hope it's nice and calm.

Patient 8 rushes in. Their ears are terribly red.

Receptionist	Good morning. Goodness gracious. What happened to your ears?
Patient 8	Well, I was ironing my best skirt/shirt when the phone rang.
Receptionist	What has this got to do with your ears?
Patient 8	Well, I answered the phone with what I was holding in my hand.
Receptionist	Oh, I see. But, but what about the other ear?
Patient 8	Well, I had to ring you to make an appointment with the doctor, didn't I?
Patient 1	(*rushing in with long canine teeth*) Good morning.
Receptionist	Hello, again. What can I do for you?
Patient 1	(*to patient with red ears*) You have such a wonderful neck.
Patient 8	What? Help!

Patient 1 bites Patient 8. Doctor and Nurse rush out of the surgery into reception.

Doctor	What have you done?!
Patient 1	Sorry, I suddenly felt very hungry.
Doctor	(*to receptionist*) Call the police!
Nurse	And the bat catcher!
Patient 1	Bye, everyone, I won't wait for them.
Doctor	And then call the ambulance.
Receptionist	For this poor patient?
Doctor	No not for them.

Short sketches

Nurse	Then for who?
Doctor	Us! What a week!
Receptionist	(*pointing to audience.*) What about this lot?
Doctor	They'll have to come back another time.

They all faint.

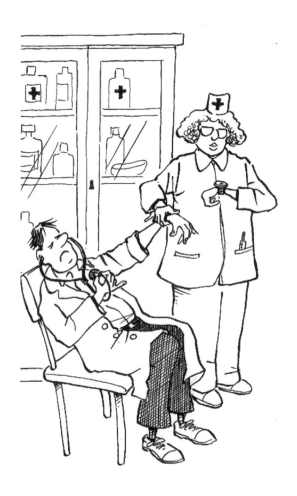

Chapter 2
Medium-length sketches

Medium-length sketches

On Holiday in Rome

A parody sketch in 4 scenes

CD Track 09

Roles	9–14 (if the 3 narrator roles and the roles for Mr and Mrs Davies are doubled)
Runtime	Around 10 minutes, depending on production
Sets	A small seaside B&B in the south of England; a street in that town; the lobby of a hotel in Rome
Props	A handkerchief, a key, 2 hamburgers, 3 chairs to make a seaside bench, a newspaper, a small suitcase; a poster advertising the lottery reading: *Summer lottery. Win £1,000,000. Last day! Don't miss your chance!*; a suit for the lottery representative; a cheque for £1,000,000; a banner, *Benvenuti a Roma*, indicating that this is a hotel in Rome; a big suitcase; 3 umbrellas
Style	A parody sketch on England and holidays in a British seaside town, drawing on a number of cultural clichés about what is 'typically British'
Synopsis	Mr and Mrs Davies are spending their holidays in Bournemouth … just as they have done every summer for more than 20 years. It's a typical holiday in a typical B&B in a typical British summer – but things suddenly change as the Davieses decide to buy a lottery ticket …
Language level	Intermediate – B1
Language areas	Everyday English phrases (high frequency chunks of language), e.g. *It's so good to see you again. / It's so good to be back. / like every year / That's absolutely OK. / This burger is delicious. – It is indeed. / I was so hungry. – So was I. / a bite to eat / You mean we could see the …? – We certainly could. / What is it about? / I'm afraid I can't tell you. / That's unbelievable. /* Tag questions (*It's our room, isn't it? That would be fantastic, wouldn't it?*)
Stage tips	This is a slightly longer play than the other pieces in this book so far. So it might be advisable to double the roles of the narrators (and Mr and Mrs Davies could also be doubled). If you are planning to do so, please bear in mind that each of the actors to be doubled should be wearing a typical piece of clothing. When the respective actor goes off, and their successor comes on stage, they should be wearing the same piece of clothing so that it is easier for the audience to understand that although the actors have changed the roles remain the same.

Materials

Photocopiable Worksheet A p 196
- Comprehension check
- Use of tenses
- Vocabulary: in the restaurant

Photocopiable Worksheet B p 197
- Dialogue
- Tag questions
- Creative writing: a friend's visit

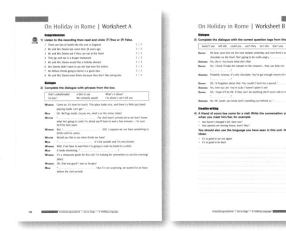

Medium-length sketches

On Holiday in Rome

Track 09

Roles Narrators 1–3
Mr Davies
Mrs Davies
Ms Wilson, landlady
Lottery Representative, wearing a smart suit
Hotel Receptionists 1 and 2

Scene 1 A small seaside B&B in the south of England

The three narrators enter (maybe carrying suitcases and wearing macks.)

NARRATOR 1 Hello everyone, and welcome to this play …

NARRATOR 2 … which we have set in a typical British seaside town.

NARRATOR 3 Typical British costume! *(puts on head a handkerchief knotted at all 4 corners)*

NARRATOR 1 Typical British weather! *(puts up umbrella)*

NARRATOR 2 Typical British seaside fun!

Narrators 1 & 3 make seagull sounds, Narrator 2 looks happily at the sky, then mimes getting seagull poop in his/her eye.

ALL THREE Yuck!

NARRATOR 2 In a minute you're going to meet Mr and Mrs Davies.

NARRATOR 3 They're a lovely couple, as you will see, and you should know that right now …

NARRATOR 1 … Mr and Mrs Davies are on their holidays.

NARRATOR 2 This is a typical small seaside hotel,

Narrator 2 moves to a table and sits down as though he/she is a guest in the hotel.

NARRATOR 3 near a place called Bournemouth

Narrator 3 joins Narrator 2 at the table

NARRATOR 1 in the south of England.

Narrator 1 joins the other two at the table.

NARRATOR 2 And in fact, Mr and Mrs Davies have come to this place for their holidays …

NARRATOR 3 … for more than 20 years.

NARRATOR 1 They know it well, and of course they know their landlady well.

NARRATOR 2 And here they come, Mr and Mrs Davies …

NARRATOR 3 … and the landlady, Ms Wilson.

Enter Mr and Mrs Davies from one side, and Ms Wilson from the other

MS WILSON Welcome back, Mr Davies, Mrs Davies. It's so good to see you again.

Medium-length sketches

MR DAVIES	Oh, thank you, Ms Wilson. It's so good to be back.
MRS DAVIES	How have you been?
MS WILSON	Oh, just fine, you know. We've had some lovely weather recently.
MR DAVIES	Yes, we saw that on TV — only three days' rain last week!
MRS DAVIES	We couldn't wait to get back here again, could we, darling?
MR DAVIES	Yes, that's right, dear! So lovely to be back.
MS WILSON	Well, let me give you your key. It's Room 4 on the first floor, like every year.
MR DAVIES	That's great. Room 4 again. It's our room, isn't it, sweetheart?
MRS DAVIES	Yes, it is! And it always feels just like home.
MS WILSON	That's lovely! I hope you enjoy the stay. See you tomorrow at breakfast, then.
MR DAVIES	Right. Erm … we wanted to ask you a favour, Ms Wilson.
MS WILSON	Certainly. What is it?
MRS DAVIES	We're a bit hungry. Is there any chance we can get something to eat? We're a bit peckish really. From the long train ride, you see.
MS WILSON	I'm so sorry, but it's 6.35, and we don't serve food after 6.30. Remember! Breakfast from 7.00 until 8.00, lunch from 1.00 until 2.00 and dinner from 5.30 until 6.30.
MR DAVIES	Sure. No problem. Sorry for asking.
MS WILSON	That's fine, don't worry. I'm sorry we can't serve you anything right now.
MRS DAVIES	That's absolutely OK. We'll see you in the morning then.
MS WILSON	That's right. Have a good rest.
MR AND MRS DAVIES	Thank you.
NARRATOR 1	Mr and Mrs Davies are really happy to be back in their lovely little holiday place,
	Narrator 1 moves chair from table to somewhere else facing audience.
NARRATOR 2	but they are still hungry so after they have taken the luggage to their room,
	Narrator 2 moves his/her chair next to Narrator 1.
NARRATOR 3	they decide it would be the right time to go for a little walk and get a bite to eat.
	Narrator 3 adds his/her chair to other two to form a 'seaside bench'.
NARRATOR 1	And here they are …
NARRATOR 2	We can see them in the streets of Bournemouth enjoying a lovely burger.
	Narrators, in unison, sit on their 'bench' and mime opening a newspaper and reading it.

Scene 2   A street

MR DAVIES	This burger is delicious!

Medium-length sketches

MRS DAVIES	It is indeed. It's the best burger ...
MR DAVIES	... we've had for a long time.
MRS DAVIES	I was so hungry!
MR DAVIES	Yes, I know. So was I!
MRS DAVIES	I think we should leave home a bit earlier next year.
MR DAVIES	Yes, that's right. We shouldn't have got here after 6.30.
MRS DAVIES	No, we shouldn't ... Then we can still get a bite to eat in our lovely little hotel.

Narrators, in unison, drop newspaper from in front of their faces.

NARRATOR 1	And while Mr and Mrs Davies are walking the streets of Bournemouth
NARRATOR 2	enjoying a lovely hamburger,
NARRATOR 3	they suddenly see something that's going to change their lives.
MR DAVIES	Look at that!
MRS DAVIES	*Summer Lottery. Win £1,000,000. Last day. Don't miss your chance!*
MR DAVIES	Wow! That would be fantastic, wouldn't it? If we won that money, we could come to Bournemouth twice a year.
MRS DAVIES	Indeed, and we could do much more. We could travel wherever we wanted. To Rome for example!
MR DAVIES	To Rome? You mean we could see the Colosseum?
MRS DAVIES	We certainly could. And St. Peter's.
MR DAVIES	St. Peter's? I've always wanted to see that.
MRS DAVIES	Me too. And we could ... (*he suddenly starts walking faster*) ... where are you going?
MR DAVIES	I'm going to buy a lottery ticket. It's the last day.
MRS DAVIES	Not so fast. Wait for me!
MR DAVIES	Hurry up! We don't want to miss our chance.

Scene 3   **Back at the B&B**

NARRATOR 1	(*bringing chair back to table*) It's now a week later,
NARRATOR 2	(*bringing chair back to table*) and as Mr and Mrs Davies are coming down for breakfast
NARRATOR 3	(*bringing chair back to table*) in their lovely little hotel
NARRATOR 1	in Bournemouth
NARRATOR 2	in the south of England,
NARRATOR 3	something unexpected happens.

Medium-length sketches

Narrators mime breakfast activities – bashing a soft-boiled egg with a teaspoon, pouring tea, buttering toast. Maybe one can ask another to 'Pass the marmalade, please'.

Enter lottery representative.

Lottery rep	Good morning.
Ms Wilson	Good morning. I'm sorry, we're full.
Lottery rep	That's fine. I don't want a room, I want to speak to one of your guests.
Ms Wilson	Oh, really? What's it about?
Lottery rep	I'm afraid I can't tell you. Are Mr and Mrs Davies in?
Mr and Mrs Davies	(*coming down the stairs*) That's us. What is it?
Lottery rep	Mr Davies. Mrs Davies. Good morning. (*quietly, so that the landlady cannot hear it. She is a bit nosey, though, and doesn't leave the room.*) I've got some good news for you.
Mrs Davies	Good news?
Lottery rep	(*very quietly*) You've won the lottery!
Mrs Davies	(*shouting*) We've won the lottery! I can't believe it! That's £1,000,000!
Ms Wilson	Oh, that's fantastic! Congratulations! Shall I book you in for next year?
Mrs Davies	Errrr … (*realising she's let the cat out of the bag*)
Lottery rep	Here's your cheque. £1,000,000! Could you sign here, please?
Mr Davies	£1,000,000. That's unbelievable!
Mrs Davies	Now we can even go to Rome!

Exit the Davieses and the lottery rep.

Ms Wilson	(*to Narrators*) Rome! What's Rome got that Bournemouth hasn't?! (*Exit*)

Scene 4	**The lobby of a hotel in Rome**
Narrator 1	So all that happened half a year ago
Narrator 2	and it took Mr and Mrs Davies a long time to fully understand
Narrator 3	that they were now the proud owners of £1,000,000.
Narrator 1	But one day Mr and Mrs Davies thought it was time …
Narrator 2	(*takes off handkerchief hat and mack*) to enjoy the money that they had won …
Narrator 3	(*takes off handkerchief hat and mack*) and they decided …
Narrator 1	(*takes off handkerchief hat and mack*) to go to Rome for a holiday.

All 3 narrators put on sunglasses at the same time and say 'Ciao' to the audience in unison with accompanying 'Italian' gesture.

Narrator 2	And here they are, just checking into their hotel.
Receptionist 1	Good evening, and welcome to the Plaza Hotel.

Medium-length sketches

Mr Davies	Good evening.
Mrs Davies	Good evening.
Receptionist 1	Your name, please?
Mr Davies	Davies.
Receptionist 1	Mr and Mrs Davies. Just a moment … all right. Here we are. Your booking is for a double room and all meals for a week.
Mrs Davies	That's right.
Receptionist 1	All right. That's room 1209 on the 12th floor. The lift's over there and the porter will bring the luggage to your room. (*clicks fingers*)

One of the narrators acts as the porter and approaches the couple.

Mr Davies	Thank you, but that's not necessary.
Receptionist 1	As you wish, sir.

Porter returns to others, muttering pretend Italian complaints about 'Inglesi'.

Mr Davies	Let's hurry, darling. I'm so hungry.
Receptionist 2	Our restaurant is on the first floor.
Mrs Davies	The restaurant? At this time of the evening? It's quarter to 8. Surely the restaurant isn't still open?
Mr Davies	Yes, we were just thinking of getting a hamburger somewhere. The restaurant must be closed.
Receptionist 2	No, sir, madam, really. The restaurant is open from 7.30 to 11. You can take your time and enjoy a lovely meal with a view of St. Peter's.
Mrs Davies	7.30 to 11! What are the times of the other meals then?
Receptionist 1	We serve breakfast from 7 to 11.30,
Receptionist 2	we serve lunch from 12 to half past 3 in the afternoon,
Receptionist 1	we serve tea from 4 to 6 o'clock, and as we've said …
Receptionist 2	… dinner is from 7.30 to 11.
Mr Davies	Ah, all right. Just a moment, please.

He turns to his wife, and they have a conversation, but we can't hear what they are saying. Apparently there is something they're not happy about.

Mrs Davies	Erm … (*coughing*) … my husband and I have decided we can't stay in this hotel.
Receptionist 1	Oh, I'm really sorry, madam, sir. We are doing everything we can to please our guests.
Mr Davies	No, sorry – we've decided to leave straightaway!
Receptionist 2	We're dreadfully sorry, sir! Could we learn what has suddenly upset you?
Mrs Davies	You serve breakfast from 7 to half past 11 …
Receptionist 1	Yes!

Medium-length sketches

MR DAVIES	Lunch from 12 to half past 3 in the afternoon?
RECEPTIONIST 2	Absolutely!
MRS DAVIES	Tea from 4 to 6 in the afternoon.
RECEPTIONIST 1	That's right!
MR DAVIES	And dinner from 7.30 to 11.
RECEPTIONIST 2	Indeed.
MRS DAVIES	That's 14 hours!
RECEPTIONIST 1	That's right. But I don't understand.
MRS DAVIES	You don't understand?
RECEPTIONIST 1	We're really sorry, madam. We fail to see what …
MR DAVIES	(*counting on his fingers*) 14 hours! We've come here to see the sights of Rome!
RECEPTIONISTS	Yes?
MRS DAVIES	But you just want us to stay in your hotel for 14 hours every day,
MR DAVIES	and eat, eat and eat. Sorry, we don't want that.
RECEPTIONISTS	But …
MR DAVIES	Come on, dear.
MR & MRS DAVIES	Bournemouth, here we come!

They put their umbrellas up and storm out. The receptionists are left with their mouths wide open.

NARRATORS	(*after a moment's hesitation*) Wait for us! (*They charge off as well.*)

Medium-length sketches

12 At the Hairdresser's

A comedy sketch in 1 scene

Roles	4*–6
	(*if Customer 1 doubles as Knuckles and Customer 2 doubles as Police Officer)
Runtime	Around 12 minutes, depending on production
Set	A hairdresser's shop
Props	3 customer's chairs; combs, hairdryers, scissors, shampoos, hairsprays and conditioners, a hand-held mirror, a swimming cap with a hole in it and 2 single hairs protruding through it (made of thick wool so that they're easily visible to the audience); a felt-tip pen; poster paper (for the Young Woman to create a poster during the play); a pop magazine; a swag bag for Knuckles Murphy
Style	A comedy sketch that shows how ridiculous vanity can be
Synopsis	It's hard times for an old hairdresser who gets hardly any customers in his shop. When a young woman stops by to ask for a job, he feels he has to turn her down as he hasn't got enough work to keep himself busy, let alone her as well. But the young lady is creative, and turns his business round.
Language level	Intermediate – B1
Language areas	Present Perfect (*I haven't had a single customer all day./I've been a hairdresser for 30 years./I've seen your sign*); *If*-clauses (*If you give me a job, I'll show you./If that happens, you'll go to prison./He would if he came here./If you had let him in, we would have made more money*); *Will*-future (*You'll be a real hit with the ladies!*)
Stage tips	There are at least two scenes where miming skills are very important: when the assistant does the hair of the bald customer, and when the hairdresser attends to the man who wants to look like a pop star. These scenes in particular need to be practised in such a way that the actors learn to see what they are doing 'through the eyes of the audience'; for example, when the assistant is combing the two hairs that stick out of the first customer's swimming cap, this needs to be done slowly and exaggeratedly, with the two hairs being held up high between the assistant's fingers, so that the audience can see them clearly.
	In the middle section of the play, when the second customer wants to look like a pop star, it's advisable to change the names of stars and bands shown in angle brackets (see below) to others that are better known to your students. It shouldn't be too difficult for students to come up with names that are up to date!

Medium-length sketches

YOUNG WOMAN   Would you like your hair cut like <Robbie Williams>?

CUSTOMER 2   Well, it's not bad, but maybe a bit too curly.

YOUNG WOMAN   How about <Will Young>?

CUSTOMER 2   No, his hair's too short.

YOUNG WOMAN   How about <Jonas Altberg>?

CUSTOMER 2   No, his hair's too straight. (*etc*)

Variations   The dialogue as shown above could be extended much more; students could add further stars (maybe not only from the world of pop, but also sports players, film stars, politicians etc).

Materials

Photocopiable Worksheet A p 198
- Comprehension check
- Vocabulary: idiomatic phrases
- Deciding what to do

Photocopiable Worksheet B p 199
- *if*-clauses
- Present perfect
- Creative writing: a job application

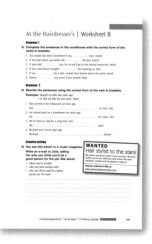

Medium-length sketches

At the Hairdresser's

Roles **Hairdresser**
A young woman
Customer 1: he is bald (see props, p 96)
Customer 2: (another young man)
Knuckles Murphy, the bank robber
A police officer

The hairdresser, an elderly man, is in his shop, waiting for customers. He is rather frustrated, as nobody is turning up.

HAIRDRESSER This is terrible! It's 5 o'clock. I haven't had a single customer this afternoon. Well, I haven't had a single customer all day. In fact, I've been a hairdresser for 30 years, and people don't want my haircuts any more. I don't know what's going wrong. I might as well shut the shop early and go home.

The door opens; enter Young Woman.

HAIRDRESSER (*aside*) Oh, it's a customer. (*to the young woman*) Good evening.
YOUNG WOMAN Good evening.
HAIRDRESSER Would you like a haircut?
YOUNG WOMAN No. I wouldn't.
HAIRDRESSER (*aside*) Oh, dear!
YOUNG WOMAN I don't want a haircut. I want a job.
HAIRDRESSER You want a job?
YOUNG WOMAN Yes, as a hairdresser.
HAIRDRESSER I can't give you a job. I haven't got enough work to keep myself busy.
YOUNG WOMAN Ah, that's where I can help.
HAIRDRESSER You? What do you mean?
YOUNG WOMAN Well, if you give me a job, I'll show you.
HAIRDRESSER There's no point. You can't get me any customers.
YOUNG WOMAN Well, your problem is that you need to be more creative. Then you'll get some customers.
HAIRDRESSER Nonsense! You can't get me any customers.
YOUNG WOMAN Wait and see! I'll get you three within an hour.
HAIRDRESSER I'll tell you what. If you can get me three customers in an hour, I'll eat my hat.
YOUNG WOMAN Deal!
HAIRDRESSER Deal!

The young woman starts to leave the shop.

HAIRDRESSER Where are you going?
YOUNG WOMAN I'm going to get you a customer.

Medium-length sketches

Hairdresser	A customer? How will you do that?
Young woman	Wait and see. You've got to be creative. (*Exit*)
Hairdresser	She's mad. This'll never work. How could she ever get me a customer?

The door opens and she comes back in, with a bald customer.

Young woman	Please sit down, sir.

The hairdresser takes her aside, and talks to her quietly.

Hairdresser	What are you doing?
Young woman	What do you mean, what am I doing?
Hairdresser	Well, this man's bald.
Young woman	That's not true!
Hairdresser	It is true. He's bald!
Young woman	No … look. (*they go back to the customer*) He's got two hairs left!
Hairdresser	And?
Young woman	Well, you've got to be creative.
Hairdresser	I don't understand.
Young woman	Give me your comb.
Hairdresser	Here you are.

The young woman starts breaking the teeth off the comb.

Hairdresser	What are you doing?
Young woman	Just wait.

She turns round and produces a comb with just one tooth left. Then she starts combing the customer's head.

Young woman	How would you like it done, sir?
Customer 1	I don't really know.
Young woman	Well, may I suggest one on the left, and one on the right? (*she does it*) How's that?
Customer 1	Fantastic!
Young woman	You'll be a real hit with the ladies, sir.
Customer 1	D'you think so?
Young woman	I certainly do!
Customer 1	Excuse me …
Young woman	Yes?
Customer 1	Could I have some hairspray? It's a bit windy outside; I don't want to ruin my beautiful new hairdo.

Medium-length sketches

YOUNG WOMAN Certainly, sir! Very wise, sir. (*she turns to the hairdresser*) Give me the spray, please.

HAIRDRESSER Here you are.

YOUNG WOMAN Thank you. (*she starts spraying*)
(*to the hairdresser*) Can you get me the mirror?

HAIRDRESSER The mirror? What do you want it for?

YOUNG WOMAN I want to show Sir the back.

HAIRDRESSER Are you crazy?

YOUNG WOMAN Trust me. Give me a felt-tip pen.

HAIRDRESSER A felt-tip pen? What for?

YOUNG WOMAN You've got to be creative. Wait and see.

Hairdresser hands a felt-tip pen to the young woman. She starts drawing a few hairs in straight lines on the mirror.

YOUNG WOMAN Have a look, sir. How do you like the back?

CUSTOMER 1 It's fantastic! I'm so happy. It's the best hairdo I've had for ages. How much do I owe you?

YOUNG WOMAN (*to the hairdresser*) How much is it?

HAIRDRESSER (*to the customer, rather quietly*) Four pounds fif …

YOUNG WOMAN (*interrupting him*) You've got to be creative! (*raising her voice*) Fourteen pounds fifty, sir.

Hairdresser looks shocked.

CUSTOMER 1 £14.50? That's a bargain! Here's £20. Keep the change.

YOUNG WOMAN Thank you very much, sir.

Exit Customer 1.

YOUNG WOMAN I told you! You've got to be creative.

HAIRDRESSER Fine. You've got us one customer. But what next?

YOUNG WOMAN I told you! You've got to be creative.

HAIRDRESSER What do you mean?

YOUNG WOMAN Well, give me the felt-tip pen again.

HAIRDRESSER What are you doing?

YOUNG WOMAN I'm writing a sign. (*she writes a big poster*)

HAIRDRESSER What does it say?

YOUNG WOMAN (*showing him the poster*) Look!

HAIRDRESSER (*reading aloud*) 'Get your hair cut like a pop star!' That's crazy!

YOUNG WOMAN Wait and see.

Medium-length sketches

She puts up the sign on the stage, so that it is visible to the audience. A short while later a young man walks by, headphones on, humming or whistling. He sees the sign, and enters the shop. He is Customer 2.

CUSTOMER 2	Good afternoon.
YOUNG WOMAN	Good afternoon.
HAIRDRESSER	What can we do for you?
CUSTOMER 2	I've seen your sign. I'd like my hair cut like a pop star.
YOUNG WOMAN	Very well, sir. *(takes out a magazine and shows it to the customer)* Would you like your hair cut like <Robbie Williams>?
CUSTOMER 2	Well, it's not bad, but maybe a bit too curly.
YOUNG WOMAN	How about <Will Young>?
CUSTOMER 2	No, his hair's too short.
YOUNG WOMAN	How about <Jonas Altberg>?
CUSTOMER 2	No, his hair's too straight.
YOUNG WOMAN	Well, tell me then, which pop star's hair do you like?
CUSTOMER 2	Can you make me look like <Slash> from <Guns N' Roses>?
YOUNG WOMAN	Well I can't, but my colleague's an expert on <Guns N' Roses>.
HAIRDRESSER	*(to young woman)* What? I don't even know who they are.
YOUNG WOMAN	*(whispering to the hairdresser)* Just be creative, and leave the rest to me. *(to the customer, more loudly)* Would you please sit down over there?
HAIRDRESSER	*(quietly, to the young woman)* What shall I do?
YOUNG WOMAN	Be creative. Get cutting!

The hairdresser starts doing the customer's hair with trembling hands, then becomes more and more confident.

HAIRDRESSER	Some to the left, some to the right. A bit of spray. *(draws a few lines on a mirror, and holds the mirror behind the customer's head)* There you go!
CUSTOMER 2	What do you mean, There you go?
HAIRDRESSER	I've finished. A haircut like <Slash>.
CUSTOMER 2	But it's terrible!
HAIRDRESSER	Terrible? What do you mean?
CUSTOMER 2	It's awful!
HAIRDRESSER	What do you mean?
YOUNG WOMAN	Is there a problem, sir?

Medium-length sketches

Customer 2	(*really desperate*) Yes. It's the ugliest haircut in the world. <Slash> doesn't have his hair cut like this!
Young woman	No, I know, but he *would* if he came *here*.
Customer 2	Ah. I see. Of course!
Young woman	Do you understand, sir?
Customer 2	Yes, I do. That's very creative. How much do I owe you?
Hairdresser	Four ...
Young woman	... ty-five pounds fifty, sir.
Customer 2	£45.50? That's a bargain! Here's £50.
Young woman	Thank you, sir.
Customer 2	Thanks. Bye!

Exit Customer 2.

Hairdresser	This is brilliant! How much have we got?
Young woman	Well the bald man gave us £20, and that man gave us £50, so we've already made £70.
Hairdresser	That's fantastic! That's more than I normally make in a week!
Young woman	See? What did I tell you?
Hairdresser	But you promised me three customers.
Young woman	Just you wait and see.
Hairdresser	Well, I close in five minutes – it's five to six. How are you going to do that?
Young woman	Here comes the third.

The door opens; enter Knuckles Murphy, wearing a cap and mask, and carrying a bag marked SWAG.)

Hairdresser	Good evening, sir. Can we help you?
Knuckles Murphy	(*politely*) Yes.
Young woman	See? I told you.
Knuckles Murphy	(*adopting a pantomime-style threatening posture*) Put up your hands, and hand over the money!
Young woman	How on *earth* are we supposed to do that?
Hairdresser	Don't you recognise him? He's Knuckles Murphy, the famous bank robber. His picture's all over the town. Give him the money.
Young woman	No!
Hairdresser	*Give him the money!*
Young woman	*No!*
Hairdresser	What do you mean, No?
Young woman	Just wait. You've got to be creative!

Medium-length sketches

KNUCKLES MURPHY   Stop talking and give me the money!

YOUNG WOMAN   You are Knuckles Murphy, aren't you, sir?

KNUCKLES MURPHY   Yeah! So?

YOUNG WOMAN   The famous bank robber?

KNUCKLES MURPHY   Yeah! *So?*

YOUNG WOMAN   Your picture's all over the town.

KNUCKLES MURPHY   Yeah! *So?*

YOUNG WOMAN   Well, that's a problem. Sooner or later, the police will recognise you. If that happens, you'll go to prison.

KNUCKLES MURPHY   I *know*! But what can I do?

YOUNG WOMAN   Well I think we can help you.

KNUCKLES MURPHY   How?

YOUNG WOMAN   Wait and see! (*aside*) You've got to be creative. (*to Knuckles Murphy*) Please sit down here, sir.

KNUCKLES MURPHY   OK – but no funny business!

YOUNG WOMAN   Right. Take off your cap.

KNUCKLES MURPHY   Knuckles Murphy never takes off his cap.

YOUNG WOMAN   Trust me. You've got to be creative.

KNUCKLES MURPHY   OK, but I'm warning you – no funny business!

YOUNG WOMAN   Just relax. (*quietly, to the hairdresser*) Come on, we've got to work fast.

HAIRDRESSER   Some to the left, some to the right.

YOUNG WOMAN   And a bit of spray.

HAIRDRESSER   There you go.

A police officer enters the shop. He/she is out of breath.

POLICE OFFICER   Good evening!

BOTH   Good evening, officer. Can we help you?

POLICE OFFICER   Yes, we've heard that Knuckles Murphy, the famous bank robber, ran in here just a few minutes ago. Have you seen him?

YOUNG WOMAN   No, I haven't.

POLICE OFFICER   Have you seen Knuckles Murphy?

HAIRDRESSER   No, I haven't, officer.

POLICE OFFICER   (*to Knuckles Murphy*) And how about you, sir? Have you seen Knuckles Murphy?

KNUCKLES MURPHY   No, I haven't. I'm really sorry, officer.

POLICE OFFICER   Well, I'd better be off then. Knuckles Murphy must be caught. (*He runs off, then stops in the doorway, and turns to Knuckles Murphy.*) Oh, by the way …

Medium-length sketches

Knuckles Murphy	What is it, officer?
Police officer	Lovely haircut, if you don't mind me saying so.
Knuckles Murphy	Thank you!

Exit police officer.

Knuckles Murphy	Crikey, I don't believe it! He didn't recognise me!
Young woman	Didn't I tell you, sir?
Hairdresser	You've got to be creative.
Knuckles Murphy	That's right! How much do I owe you?
Young woman	Four ...
Hairdresser	... hundred and fifty pounds.
Knuckles Murphy	£450? That's a bargain! (*he takes the money out of his swag bag and gives it to the young woman*) That's £500. Keep the change.
Young woman	Thank you, sir.
Knuckles Murphy	Bye!
Hairdresser and young woman	Bye!

Exit Knuckles.

Young woman	See?
Hairdresser	How much have we made?
Young woman	Well, we've got £20 and £50, plus £500 from Knuckles Murphy. That makes £570.
Hairdresser	£570 – that's more than I make in a year!
Young woman	What did I tell you?
Both	*You've got to be creative!*
Hairdresser	Precisely.

The door opens. The police officer is back. They're a bit shocked.

Police officer	Hold on a minute, you two!
Hairdresser	Yes, officer?
Police officer	I want a word with you.
Both	What about?
Police officer	I just wanted to know ...
Both	Yes?
Police officer	Whether you could cut my hair like the man I saw just now.
Hairdresser	I'm sorry ...
Police officer	What's the problem?
Hairdresser	I'm sorry. We're closed. Come back tomorrow!

Police officer	OK. (*Exit*)
Young woman	Why did you send him away? If you'd let him in, we'd have made more money!
Hairdresser	We've been creative enough for one day.
Young woman	That's true. And anyhow …
Hairdresser	What?
Young woman	You need time to eat your hat now.

Medium-length sketches

13 The Space Restaurant

A comedy sketch in 1 scene

Note In this play, people are in a restaurant where they order pork or beef from the menu. If you are teaching in a country where eating pork or beef is unacceptable, please change to something culturally more appropriate, for example, fish.

Roles 13 (If you want more actors, you may want to add more customers, or to double longer roles, e.g. Luigi's. If needed, the cast can also be reduced, by having just 4 customers who are very thirsty/hungry, each of them ordering 2 drinks/meals)

Runtime Around 10 minutes, depending on production

Set In a restaurant

Props 4 tables with 2 chairs each for the customers to sit at; black trousers, white shirts, and a white cloth for each of the waiters; various props for the tourists (to be chosen by your students, e.g. camera, Bermuda shirt, sunglasses etc.).

Sticky labels, a felt-tip pen, a menu; a vase with (artificial) flowers that's big enough to contain the contents of 8 glassfuls, several (plastic) glasses; 8 very small plates; colourful 'pills' (sweets such as Smarties or M&Ms) that the students can really eat.

The costumes for the astronauts can be made by covering crash helmets (if available) with silver foil. Use boxes of different sizes to cover the astronauts' bodies and arms – again, stick foil on them; use wire to make their antennae.

Style A comedy sketch using slapstick and situational humour

Synopsis Four couples – all of them tourists – end up in a restaurant that seems rather unusual at first sight: a waitress who can't remember what the guests have ordered; very small plates, and no cutlery. But as the story unfolds, our customers become happier and happier, maybe also because of Luigi, the cunning restaurant owner.

Language level Intermediate – B1

Language areas Ordering food and drink (*I'll have a lemonade*); possessive pronouns

Vocabulary: food and drink

Stage tips Show the students the recording of the play on the DVD to prepare them for the acting. As teenagers usually love imitating other teens, it should be easy to get your students to try and imitate the actors they see on the DVD.

Medium-length sketches

Materials

Photocopiable Worksheet A p 200
- Comprehension check
- Vocabulary: food
- In a restaurant

Photocopiable Worksheet B p 201
- Possessive pronouns
- Use of tenses
- Creative writing: in a restaurant

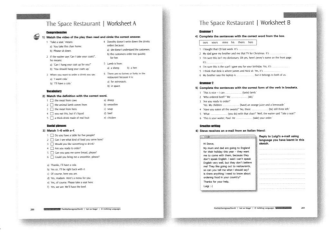

Medium-length sketches

 ## The Space Restaurant

Roles Luigi, the restaurant owner
Manuel, waiter
Dorothy, waitress
Customers 1–8 (clearly tourists)

LUIGI (*to audience*) Good evening, ladies and gentlemen, and welcome to the Space Restaurant here in London. This is my waiter, Manuel, and here is my waitress, Dorothy.

Manuel and Dorothy bow to the audience.

LUIGI It's getting very exciting today, because we have a party of people coming from abroad. Their English isn't very good, and they're in a hurry. But that's no problem – we're the Space Restaurant. *(Doorbell rings)* And here they come right now!

Luigi notices that two guests are trying to get in, but they can't as the door is locked.

LUIGI Oh dear, the door's locked.

He opens the door; two customers come in and he closes and locks the door behind them.

CUSTOMERS 1 & 2 Good evening.

LUIGI Good evening, sir, madam.

Doorbell rings again.

LUIGI Oh dear, the door. Manuel, the door, please.

He opens the door, the next two customers come in; he locks the door again.

CUSTOMERS 3 & 4 Good evening.

MANUEL Good evening, ladies.

Doorbell rings again.

LUIGI Oh dear, the door. Dorothy? …

He opens the door, the next two customers come in; he locks the door again.

CUSTOMERS 5 & 6 Good evening.

DOROTHY Good evening, sir, madam.

Doorbell rings again. Next two customers knock at the door.

LUIGI Oh, there are still two left.

He opens the door, the last two guests come in; he locks the door again.

CUSTOMERS 7 & 8 Good evening.

Medium-length sketches

Luigi	Good evening, sir, madam. (*he leads them to their tables*)
Luigi	(*to Customers 1 and 2*) Please sir, madam, take a seat.

Customers 1 & 2 each grab a chair and start to walk off with it.

Luigi	Stop! What are you doing?
Customers 1 & 2	We're taking a seat. You said 'Take a seat'.
Luigi	No! Here in England 'Take a seat' means 'Sit down'.
Customers 1 and 2	Ah, thank you!

All the customers sit down, except Customers 3 & 4, who sit on the floor.

Dorothy	What are you doing?
Customers 3 & 4	We're sitting down. He said 'sit down' (*points towards floor.*)
Dorothy	No, here in England 'sit down' means 'sit on a chair'.
Customers 3 & 4	Ah, thank you!
Manuel	(*to Customers 5 & 6, who are sitting with their coats on*) Can I take your coats?
Customers 5 & 6	Our coats? No, you can't. They're ours.
Luigi	No! Here in England 'Can I take your coats?' means 'Can I hang up your coats?'
Customer 5 & 6	(*hand him their coats*) Ah, thank you. Here you are.
Luigi	Dorothy will take your drinks orders.
Customer 1	I'll have an apple juice.
Customer 2	I'll have a cola.
Customer 3	I'll have a lemonade.
Customer 4	I'll have a soda.
Customer 5	I'll have a cup of tea.
Customer 6	I'll have a coffee.
Customer 7	I'll have an orange juice.
Customer 8	And I'll have a smoothie.
Dorothy	(*panicking as she can't remember what they've ordered*) Sorry, that was too quick! I can't remember …
Customer 1	I'll have an apple juice.
Customer 2	I'll have a cola.
Customer 3	I'll have a lemonade.
Customer 4	I'll have a soda.
Customer 5	I'll have a cup of tea.
Customer 6	I'll have a coffee.
Customer 7	I'll have an orange juice.
Customer 8	And I'll have a smoothie.

Medium-length sketches

Dorothy Sorry, that was still too quick, I can't write it down.

Luigi Oh, dear! Listen. (*he takes sticky labels and a marker pen, writes numbers 1–8 on the labels and puts them on the customers' fronts, chanting*)
Number one's an apple juice
Number two's a cola
Number three's a lemonade
Number four's a soda
Number five's a cup of tea
Number six is coffee
Number seven's orange juice, and
Number eight's a smoothie!

Exit Dorothy to get the drinks. Luigi or the waiter shows the menu (could be mimed if no prop available).

Manuel Ladies and gentlemen, the menu.

Customer 1 Manuel?

Manuel Yes.

Customer 1 What's 'pork'?

Manuel It's pig. Pork is pig.

Customer 2 What's 'pig'?

Manuel Pig is oink – oink – oink – oink – oink – oink. (*pig noise*)

Customer 2 Ah, I understand. Pig is oink – oink – oink – oink – oink – oink.

Luigi Yes, it is.

Customers 1 & 2 We'll have the pork.

Customer 3 Luigi?

Luigi Yes.

Customer 3 What's 'lamb'?

Luigi It's sheep. Lamb is sheep.

Customer 4 What's 'sheep'?

Luigi Sheep is baaaaaaaaaaaaaaa. (*sheep noise*)

Customer 4 Ah, I understand. Sheep is baaaaaaaaaaaaaaa.

Luigi Yes, it is.

Customers 3 & 4 We'll have the lamb.

Customer 6 Manuel?

Manuel Yes.

Customer 6 What's 'chicken'?

Manuel It's hen. Chicken is hen.

Customer 5 What's 'hen'?

Manuel Hen is cluck cluck cluck cluck cluck. (*hen noise*)

Medium-length sketches

Customer 5	Ah, I see. Hen is cluck cluck cluck cluck cluck.
Luigi	Yes, it is.
Customers 5 & 6	Ah, good. We'll have the chicken.
Customer 7	Luigi?
Luigi	Yes.
Customer 7	What's 'beef'?
Luigi	It's cow. Beef is cow.
Customer 8	What's 'cow'?
Luigi	Cow is mooooooooo. (*cow noise*)
Customer 8	Ah, I understand. Cow is mooooooooo.
Luigi	Yes, it is.
Customers 7 & 8	We'll have the beef.
All Customers	What's 'soup'?
Luigi and Manuel	(*think for a moment, but can't work out what to say*) Mmh – no soup today (*Luigi crosses the soup off all the menus*)
Manuel	OK, so that's two oink – oink – oink – oink – oink
Luigi	two baaaaaaaaaaaaaa
Manuel	two cluck cluck cluck cluck
Luigi	two mooooooooo and ... (*thinks for a moment*)
Manuel and Luigi	no soup!
Manuel	(*shouting into the kitchen*) Pork for two!
Luigi	Lamb for two!
Manuel	Chicken for two!
Luigi	Beef for two. And ...
Manuel and Luigi	no soup! (*to the customers*) We'll be right back.
	Enter Dorothy.
Dorothy	Number one's a carrot tea Two's a cabbage soda Number three's a sausage juice Four's a toothpaste cola Number five's an orange milk Six is spinach coffee Number seven's cactus juice Eight's potato smoothie.
All Customers	No, that's wrong! Listen: Number one's an apple juice Number two's a cola

Medium-length sketches

| | Number three's a lemonade
Number four's a soda
Number five's a cup of tea
Number six is coffee
Number seven's orange juice
Number eight's a smoothie. |
|---|---|
| **Dorothy** | Oh, dear. I just can't remember it. … Ah. Wait. I know! |

She takes a vase full of flowers, takes out the flowers, and pours all the drinks into it. Then she takes a spoon and triumphantly stirs the mixture.

Dorothy	There! Here's a cocktail for you.

She puts the vase on the table, then leaves. The customers look around, seeming confused.

Customer 1	She's a strange waitress.
Customer 2	Yes, and this is a very strange restaurant.
Customer 3	What do you mean?
Customer 2	Well, look at the plates.
Customer 4	The plates? What about them.
Customer 5	Oh, yes. They're tiny!
Customer 6	Oh, yes.
Customer 7	And there are no forks, no knives, no spoons … nothing to eat with.
Customer 8	Oh, yes. Very strange!

Enter Luigi, Dorothy and Manuel.

Dorothy	Ladies and gentlemen, here's your food. Who ordered beef?
Customers 7 & 8	We did.
Luigi	Beef. Here you are. (*putting a red pill on each of their plates*)
Dorothy	Who ordered chicken?
Customers 5 & 6	We did.
Manuel	Chicken. Here you are. (*putting a yellow pill on each of their plates*)
Dorothy	Who ordered lamb?
Customers 3 & 4	We did.
Luigi	Lamb. Here you are. (*putting a white pill on each of their plates*)
Dorothy	Who ordered pork?
Customers 1 & 2	We did.
Manuel	Pork. Here you are. (*putting a green pill on each of their plates*)
Customer 1	Wait a minute!
Dorothy	What's the matter?

Customer 2	We ordered food.
Dorothy	This is food.
Customer 3	No it isn't. This is a pill.
Manuel	The pill is the food!
Customer 4	What do you mean?
Luigi	This is the Space Restaurant!
Customer 5	We still don't understand!
All customers	Why do you serve pills?
Luigi	The Space Restaurant is a restaurant –
All customers	Yes?
Luigi	... for astronauts!
Dorothy & Manuel & Luigi	Enjoy your meal!

The customers start eating the pills. They look sceptical at first, but then they seem to start enjoying them.

Customers 1 & 2	I can taste pork.
Customers 3 & 4	I can taste lamb.
Customers 5 & 6	I can taste chicken.
Customers 7 & 8	I can taste beef.
All customers	Well done, Luigi!
Luigi	Thank you.
Dorothy	Dessert?
All customers	No sorry, we're full! No space.

Enter 2 astronauts.

Astronauts	Table for two, Luigi?
Luigi	No, sorry, we're full. No space!

Chapter 3

Medium-length plays based on traditional stories

Medium-length plays

14 The Wise Woman

Track 10

A short 'morality' play based on traditional story elements, in 7 scenes

Roles	14
Runtime	Around 8 minutes, depending on production
Sets	A medieval town square; outside a cottage in the town; inside the cottage; the great hall of the king's castle
Props	As many or as few props as possible given the preparation time and your students' creativity; none of the props is absolutely essential, but it would be good to have (cardboard) swords and shields for the soldiers, and a bag of gold (e.g. some nuts painted gold)
Style	A short play in a historical setting in prose, plus a rhyming chorus; the main message is about honouring the wisdom, knowledge and life experience of old people
Synopsis	When the king decides to ban old people from the town, this means a lot of pain and sorrow for old and young. But things get worse … and finally even the king understands that if it wasn't for a young boy and his mother, the country would be in serious trouble.
Language level	Intermediate – B1
Language areas	Modals – *must* (*Old people must be sent away!*)/*can't* (obligation) (*We can't do that!*)
	Unless (*He will take all the land unless we can give him one thing.*)
	Defining relative clauses (*He hates old people who can't work so hard any more./Our king is offering a reward to anyone who can bring him a drum like this one.*)
Stage tips	It will be important to explain the meaning of the chorus lines to the students, as the language used there is rather formal (like the chorus in an ancient Greek play). You can do this by getting students to read the play first. Then dictate the following sentences, and ask students to match them with the verses spoken by the chorus. They should write the chorus numbers (see script) next to the sentences below.

…… The soldiers ask the assembled people to help the king.
…… The soldiers try to find the old people and want to kill them.
…… The people think very hard, but they can't find a solution.
…… The boy builds a big cupboard with a secret place for his mother to hide in.
…… When the people hear what the king wants from them they get desperate.

...... The king is sorry for what he did, and he has sent his soldiers out to tell everybody that old people are very important because they know a lot.

...... Experience shows that knowledge is more important than physical power.

...... The king gets a task from another king – if he can't solve it, the other king's army will come.

...... The old woman tells the boy what to do, and he goes to the king to tell him.

(Key: 6 - 4 - 7 - 3 - 2 - 9 - 1 - 5 - 8)

Use the recording of the play to help your students with their pronunciation and intonation.

Materials
Track 10

Photocopiable Worksheet A p 202
- Comprehension check
- Useful phrases
- Vocabulary: formal language

Photocopiable Worksheet B p 203
- *Must* and *can't*
- Defining relative clauses
- Creative writing: an advert for a film

Medium-length plays

The Wise Woman

Roles Chorus, consisting of at least 4–6 students   Old woman
Soldiers 1–4   Her son
Men 1, 2   King
Women 1, 2   Wise men 1, 2

Prologue *Enter Chorus, marching in time and chanting.*

CHORUS (1) Listen while we tell you a tale from long ago;
Listen while we tell you of all the things we know –
Of how, when faced with cruelty, brutality and greed,
A sword and shield are not enough –
It's wisdom that you need.

CHORUS (*announcing*) Scene 1: A medieval town square

Either the chorus can continue as a separate entity, or its members can become the villagers/soldiers etc.

SOLDIER 1 People, listen to me. Our young king only wants young people in his town. Young people can work hard for him. Old people can't. Old people over 75 must go away.

MAN 1 My father is 76. Where can he go?

SOLDIER 2 Take him to the mountains.

WOMAN 1 There's no food in the mountains.

SOLDIER 3 You must do what our king says.

MAN 2 We can't do that!

SOLDIER 4 Then you'll be punished, and our king will take your houses and animals away.

WOMAN 2 That's not fair!

SOLDIER 1 Silence! Do what your king says!

CHORUS (2) Back to their homes the townsfolk go
Their souls despaired, weighed down with woe.
Some people wept, some people prayed –
But knew their king must be obeyed.

CHORUS (*announcing*) Scene 2: Outside a cottage in the town

OLD WOMAN You look sad, my son. What did the soldiers say?

SON They said old people must be sent away.

OLD WOMAN Sent away?

SON Yes – to the mountains. What can we do, Mother?

OLD WOMAN	Build a big cupboard with a secret room in it. When the soldiers come I'll hide there.
SON	I'll start right now!
CHORUS (3)	The man worked hard by day and night To get the secret room just right. But would it work? – We'll soon find out! Here come the soldiers with a shout.
CHORUS	(*announcing*) Scene 3: Inside the cottage
SON	Quickly Mother, hide! (*She does so.*)
SOLDIER 1	(*knocking*) Open up! (*Son lets the soldiers in.*) Where are your father and mother?
SON	My father's dead, and I've taken my mother to the mountains.
SOLDIER 1	Why should we believe you?
SON	If you don't, then you're welcome to search the house.
SOLDIER 2	(*to the other soldiers*) Search the house!
CHORUS (4)	They search the house, we hold our breath – Discovery means certain death! Soldiers are looking for the old … These men are scary, brutal, bold. (*The soldiers search the house.*)
SOLDIER 3	She isn't here.
SOLDIER 4	OK. Now let's go to the next house. (*Exit soldiers*)
SON	You can come out now, Mother. They've gone.
OLD WOMAN	We were lucky. I hope they won't come back.
CHORUS (5)	Some months passed by in solemn peace. But then a cruel king from the east Threatened to invade our land Unless our king met his demand – A riddle must be solved. So then Our king assembled his wise men.
CHORUS	(*announcing*) Scene 4: The king's great hall
KING	I've received bad news from the king of the country to the east. He wants all our land. He's got a mighty army that will come and take all we have unless we can give him one thing.
WISE MAN 1	And what is that thing?
KING	A drum that sounds when nobody beats it. Come, my wise men, what is the answer?
WISE MAN 2	There is no answer. It's impossible! You can't have a drum that sounds when nobody beats it.
KING	Fools! You've failed me – go away. Soldier!

Medium-length plays

SOLDIER 1	Yes, my king.
KING	Go and tell the townspeople: there's a bag of gold for whoever can bring me a drum that sounds when nobody beats it.
SOLDIER 1	Yes, my king.
CHORUS (6)	A crowd has soon assembled To hear the soldiers say What they must do to help their king Keep invaders far away.
CHORUS	(*announcing*) Scene 5: The town square
SOLDIER 1	Listen to me, everyone. The king from the country to the east wants our land. He will come with his soldiers and take your houses and animals away.
SOLDIER 2	Our brave king went to the mighty king of the east. He asked the king of the east to give our town a chance.
MAN 1	Hurrah! Our king's the best.
SON	(*aside*) I don't think so. He hates old people who can't work hard any more.
WOMAN 1	What's happened? Is the king from the east giving us a chance?
SOLDIER 3	Silence! He is. He says he won't come if we can give him a drum that sounds when nobody beats it.
WOMAN 2	Oh dear! A drum that sounds when nobody beats it …
MAN 2	That's impossible! We'll lose everything!
SOLDIER 4	Our king's offering a reward to anyone who can bring him a drum like that. A whole bag of gold! Think, everyone, think!
CHORUS (7)	They scratch their heads, they rub their chins They think and think and think … But no one finds the answer, and Their hearts begin to sink.
CHORUS	(*announcing*) Scene 6: Inside the cottage
OLD WOMAN	You look sad, my son.
SON	Mother, the king from the country to the east wants our land. He will come with his soldiers and take our houses and animals away.
OLD WOMAN	That's terrible! The king from the east is as cruel as our king.
SON	But the king from the east is giving us a chance.
OLD WOMAN	What chance?
SON	He says he won't come if we can bring him a drum that sounds when nobody beats it.
OLD WOMAN	That's easy!
SON	I don't believe you.
OLD WOMAN	Believe me, it's not difficult.
SON	But Mother, even the wise men don't know what to do!

OLD WOMAN	Maybe the wise men aren't that wise. Listen to me!
SON	All right, Mother.
OLD WOMAN	Imagine a drum with its sides made of paper. When you put a bee inside, it'll buzz around and beat against the paper with its wings. And that's the drum that sounds when nobody beats it.
CHORUS (8)	Will this be the answer? Will this save the day? The young man runs to the castle To say what he must say.
CHORUS	(*announcing*) Scene 7: The castle great hall, with everyone assembled
SON	My king, I know what we can do. We must make a drum with its sides made of paper. We must put a bee inside. The bee will buzz and beat against the paper with its wings. And that's the drum that sounds when nobody beats it!
KING	You are wiser than my wise men. Here's the bag of gold. (*to Soldier 1*) Soldier, tell the people to do what the wise young man has told us.
SOLDIER 1	Yes, my king. Straightaway!
KING	But tell me, o wise young man. Did anyone help you?
SON	My king. I cannot tell a lie. It's not me who's wise – it's my mother! I didn't send her away to the mountains. Please don't do anything to her.
KING	Your mother has saved us, so I won't send her away. I can see now that I've made a terrible mistake. From now on all the old people should be able to live in our town with their families. (*to Soldier 3*) Soldier!
SOLDIER 3	Yes, my king.
KING	Tell everyone that from now on all the old people will be able to live in our town with their families.
SOLDIER 3	I'll tell them straight away, my king.
KING	We will respect our old people, and I'm sure they'll share their wisdom with us.
	Later.
PEOPLE	Hurray! Long live the king!
CHORUS (9)	What our king says is correct – We must treat them with respect. We need the wisdom of the old – Their wisdom is worth more than gold.

Medium-length plays

15 The Reward for Kindness

A one-scene, humorous play based on a fable

Roles	7
Runtime	Around 5 minutes, depending on production
Set	Different places on a farm
Props	3 sheep's hats and cottonwool tails for the narrators (they are sheep); a big net or bed sheet; a big sausage; face paint and head gear for bear and fox; some rustic clothes for the farmer and his wife
Style	A light, fast-paced comedy sketch; the main moral lesson conveyed through the play is that dishonesty doesn't pay
Synopsis	A farmer finds a bear is killing his sheep. He sets a trap, and manages to catch it. The bear promises to show the farmer a hidden treasure if he doesn't kill him. The farmer believes him, but then finds out that he himself has been deceived by the bear, who threatens to eat him. The farmer thinks of a way out and makes an offer the bear can't refuse.
Language level	Intermediate – B1
Language areas	Expressing intention (*I'm going to kill you!/This is how I'm going to reward you.*); talking about spontaneous decisions and promises (*I'll make a trap and catch the bear./I won't kill any of your sheep any more.*) *It's time* + past tense (*It's time you gave me my reward.*)
Stage tips	An interesting idea for this play would be to use some hay bales or something that looks like hay bales. The farmer could sit on one at the beginning but then as the narrators tell the tale the bales could be moved about by the actors to create different shapes and areas. For instance, when the farmer follows the track of the bear he could simply weave in and out of three or four bales and when he sets a trap to catch the bear the bales could be stacked two high in a square with a space in the middle for the bear to fall into. They could become the henhouse, the entrance to the cottage etc. Encourage your students to experiment with the bales to create interesting and varied shapes and environments to help tell the tale of the journey.

Medium-length plays

Materials **Photocopiable Worksheet A p 204**
- Comprehension check
- Vocabulary around animals
- Expressing intentions with *going to*

Photocopiable Worksheet B p 205
- *it's time* + past tense
- Giving advice
- Creative writing: products to keep animals away

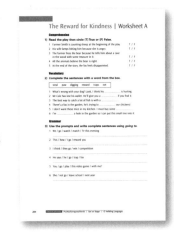

Medium-length plays

The Reward for Kindness

Roles Narrators 1–3, they are sheep (see above) Bear
Farmer Smith Fox
Hilda, the farmer's wife Old Horse
Dog

Enter Narrators 1–3 and Farmer Smith

NARRATOR 1 Farmer Smith is a sheep farmer. Here he is, counting his sheep.

FARMER 1, 2, 3, 4 ... 5 ...... 6 ...... (*falls asleep and starts snoring*)

NARRATOR 2 Now, as many of you know, counting sheep is something people use to help them go to sleep, but that's not the reason Farmer Smith is trying to count them.

FARMER (*wakes himself up suddenly with a particularly loud snore*) 1, 2, 3, 4 ... 5 ...... 6 ...... (*then falls asleep again*)

NARRATOR 3 Farmer Smith thinks a bear's killing one of his sheep every night.

NARRATOR 1 So he wants to count them to be sure.

NARRATOR 2 But, as soon as he starts counting he falls asleep.

NARRATOR 3 Luckily Farmer Smith's kind and lovely wife Hilda is here to help him.

Enter Hilda, who wakes Farmer Smith by bashing him with a large sausage.

HILDA (*bellowing*) Wakey wakey!

FARMER SMITH Thank you, my darling. What would I do without you? ... Your kindness ... and your lovely homemade sausage!

HILDA I like being kind to you, my sweetie. Carry on!

FARMER SMITH (*hastily*) 1, 2, 3 ... 4 ...... 5 (*starts to go to sleep again, but Hilda bashes him again*) ... 6, 7, 8 ... 9 ... 10 (*starts to go to sleep again but the action is repeated*) 11, 12, 13, 14 ... (*etc*)

Farmer Smith and Hilda continue to mime counting, falling asleep and bashing.

NARRATOR 1 And so the loving couple continue their work ...

NARRATOR 2 So very happy together ... (*a particularly heavy blow from Hilda's sausage*)

NARRATOR 3 Until, at last ...

FARMER SMITH 287, 288, 289. There! I knew it! That bear's taken another sheep. (*Hilda bashes him one more time.*) You can stop now, my angel.

HILDA Sorry, sweetie. What are we to do?

NARRATOR 1 The farmer looks carefully at the bear's tracks and he notices that the bear always takes the same path.

FARMER I know! I'll make a trap and catch the killer.

HILDA What can I do to help?

FARMER Go and cook that sausage, my angel. Making a trap is hungry work.

NARRATOR 2	Then, he dug a hole in the ground, put a strong net over it and covered it carefully with leaves and branches.
NARRATOR 3	Sure enough the next night the bear fell into the hole, got caught in the net and couldn't escape. When Farmer Smith came in the morning he found the bear in the net.
FARMER	Now I've got you, and I'm going to kill you!
BEAR	Farmer Smith, don't do that. Don't kill me!
FARMER	Why shouldn't I kill you? Aren't you killing my sheep?
BEAR	Let me go this time and I'll reward your kindness! I know a cave in the woods where there is some treasure. And I won't kill any of your sheep any more.
NARRATOR 1	The bear begged and begged until at last the farmer opened the net and let him out.
FARMER	Now then, let me have my reward. Show me the way to the treasure.
NARRATOR 2	The bear put a heavy paw on the farmer's shoulder.
BEAR	This is how I'm going to reward you. I'm going to eat you up!
FARMER	What? Is that what you call a reward for kindness?
BEAR	There is no reward for kindness in our world. Ask anyone and you will see I'm right.
FARMER	I don't believe it! There must be a reward for kindness.
BEAR	Very well. I'm sure I'm right. Let's go for a walk and ask the first animal or person we meet.
NARRATOR 3	The first person they met was an old horse. They told the horse the story.
OLD HORSE	The bear's right. Look at me. For thirty years I worked for a farmer. But this morning I heard him say, 'It's time we killed the old horse! He's no good for work any more.'
BEAR	What did I tell you? I was right, wasn't I! There's no reward for kindness. Now, roll up your sleeve … I think I'll start by eating one of your arms – delicious!
FARMER	No, wait! I can't believe that this is the reward kindness always gets! We must ask someone else.
BEAR	OK, but if I'm right again, I'll eat you and your wife, Hilda.
NARRATOR 1	They walked on a little farther until they met an old dog. They told him their story.
DOG	The bear's right. Look at me! I guarded my farmer's house for years, but this morning I heard him say, 'It's time we killed that old dog!' So I know that in this world there's no reward for kindness.
BEAR	You see! Now, where's the ketchup?
FARMER	No – wait! I can't believe that this is the reward kindness gets! We must ask one more person.
NARRATOR 2	The bear agreed.

Narrator 3 But only after the farmer agreed in turn that if the bear was right it could eat him, his wife AND her lovely homemade sausages!

Narrator 2 The next person they met was a fox. The fox listened carefully and then he whispered to the farmer ...

Fox (*whispering*) If I help you, will you give me all the chickens in your henhouse?

Farmer Yes, I will. Trust me!

Fox (*to bear*) Hmm! Hmm! It's difficult to say who's right. I must have a look at the place where it all happened. First, show me the sheep field.

Narrator 3 So they went to the field. The fox solemnly shook his head.

Fox It was certainly wrong of the bear to eat all those sheep! ... Now show me where you set the trap.

Narrator 1 For a long time the fox looked at the hole in the ground and the net.

Fox (*to farmer*) You say the bear got caught in this net? I want to see just how he was caught.

Farmer (*to bear*) If you want to win this bet you'll have to show him.

Narrator 2 So the bear showed the fox how he had been caught; the bear jumped into the hole and got stuck in the net. He lay there and couldn't get out.

Fox Well, you killed the sheep, so I say it's fair that the farmer's caught you. Now you can just stay there. Come on, Farmer Smith!

Narrator 3 So the fox and the farmer went away leaving the bear in the hole. When they came to the henhouse the fox stopped.

Fox I helped you. It's time you gave me my reward!

Farmer Just a moment – I must get the key to the henhouse.

Narrator 1 The farmer ran into the house and shouted to his wife.

Farmer Hilda, there's a fox outside trying to steal our chickens. Get a sausage!

Hilda does the actions below as Narrator 2 describes them.

Narrator 2 The farmer's wife grabbed the biggest, fattest sausage she could find and hurried out to the henhouse. When she found the fox she started to hit him. The fox was badly hurt, but he managed to run away.

Fox (*running away*) Now I know what reward kindness gets! Oh, what a bad, bad world this is!

16 Rusty Nail Soup

A one-scene play, based on a traditional story

Roles	10 (8 of these roles are narrators. This creates a special dramatic effect and has the extra advantage that more students can be involved in the play)
Runtime	Around 4 minutes, depending on production
Set	A country cottage
Props	A big cooking pot, a carrot, salt and pepper, a piece of meat (this could be a stone, coloured red and white as if it was meat), a carton of apple juice, glasses, a loaf of bread, 2 soup bowls and spoons
Style	A humorous play with interaction between the two main actors (an old woman and a traveller), and 8 narrators
Synopsis	When a tired and hungry traveller knocks on the door of a greedy old woman's house and asks for a place to stay for the night, she does not want to let him in. But the traveller is cunning; he shows the old woman a rusty old nail and promises to make delicious soup from it. Although she doesn't believe him at first, the offer is too tempting …
Language level	Intermediate – B1
Language areas	Future for spontaneous decisions
Stage tips	Explain to your students that the interaction between the narrators and the actors is very important. After the students have read the play for the first time, ask them to find instances of these two narrator functions in the text:

a) introducing the audience to a scene.

For example:
NARRATOR 1 Once upon a time
NARRATOR 2 in a land far away
NARRATOR 3 a poor traveller stopped in a village.
NARRATOR 1 He was cold.
NARRATOR 2 He was tired.
NARRATOR 3 He was hungry.

Medium-length plays

b) commenting on what's happening and making the action clearer to the audience.

For example:

NARRATOR 6 And having said that, the old lady tried to slam the door in his face.
NARRATOR 7 But although the man was poor, he was clever.
NARRATOR 1 He stuck his foot in the door.

Explain to the students that in order to make the interaction between narrators and actors more effective, all the actors should stay still while a narrator is speaking, and then move as directed.

The scene quoted above, for example, should be acted out in the following way:

NARRATOR 6 And having said that, the old lady tried to slam the door in his face.

While finishing the sentence, the Narrator makes a gesture inviting the audience to look at the old lady. Then, when the Narrator has finished speaking, the old lady mimes slamming the door.

NARRATOR 7 But although the man was poor, he was clever.
NARRATOR 1 He stuck his foot in the door.

Again, the Narrator makes a gesture to make the audience aware that an action is to be expected from the man. It is important that him putting his foot in the door follows immediately after Narrator 1 finishing his/her line.

Get students to watch the DVD version of the play and specifically point out to them the rhythm of the interaction between the narrators, e.g. when they say:

NARRATOR 5 The old lady wasn't sure
NARRATOR 8 but she was so curious
NARRATOR 6 she decided to let him in.

The key point here is that the three narrators speak as if they were one person, by letting their line follow the previous line without a break in between.

Let students find other examples of this type of dramatisation in the audio recording.

Materials

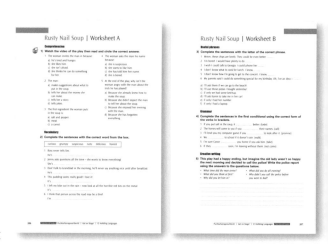

Photocopiable Worksheet A p 206
- Comprehension check
- Vocabulary: adjectives

Photocopiable Worksheet B p 207
- spontaneous decisions with *will*
- *if*-clauses
- Creative writing: a police report

Medium-length plays

 # Rusty Nail Soup

Roles Traveller
Old woman
Narrators 1–8

Scene In a country cottage

Narrator 1	Once upon a time
Narrator 2	in a land far away
Narrator 3	a poor traveller stopped in a village.
Narrator 1	He was cold.
Narrator 2	He was tired.
Narrator 3	He was hungry.
Traveller	I need food but I haven't got any money. All I have in my pocket is this rusty old nail. (*shows it to the audience*)
Narrator 4	He hoped a villager would be kind to him.
Narrator 5	So he knocked at a door. (*knock knock knock*)
Narrator 6	An old woman opened the door a tiny bit.
Old Woman	What do you want?
Traveller	Please, old woman, I'm cold and tired and hungry.
Old Woman	What do you want me to do?
Traveller	May I sleep on your floor for the night?
Old Woman	No – go away! I don't like strangers.
Narrator 6	And having said that the old lady tried to slam the door in his face.
Narrator 7	But although the man was poor, he was clever.
Narrator 1	He stuck his foot in the door.
Traveller	Wait. Please, old woman, listen to me.
Old Woman	Why should I listen to you? You're a fool! Go away.
Traveller	Because if you let me in, just to warm my feet by the fire, I will show you how to make the most delicious soup in the world from just this rusty old nail.
Old Woman	Don't talk such rubbish!
Narrator 2	But the old woman was greedy
Narrator 3	and thinking of all the money she could save if she could really make soup from a rusty nail
Narrator 4	she opened the door a little more.
Old Woman	How do I know you're not lying?
Traveller	I may be poor, but I'm an honest man.
Narrator 5	The old lady wasn't sure

Puchta/Gerngross/Devitt | Get on Stage! | © Helbling Languages **PHOTOCOPIABLE**

Medium-length plays

Narrator 8	but she was so curious
Narrator 6	she decided to let him in.
Traveller	May I sit by the fire?
Old Woman	Later. First, make the soup.
Traveller	OK. Do you have a pot?
Old Woman	Yes, I've got a pot.
Traveller	Then fill it with water and put it on the fire.
Narrator 7	Grumbling, the old woman did as she was told.

Woman mimes the actions.

Narrator 1	And while they were waiting for the water to boil,
Narrator 2	the old lady stared at the man suspiciously.
Narrator 3	But the man just smiled.
Old Woman	Look, the water's ready. What do we do now?
Traveller	It's simple. I drop the nail in the pot and we wait.
Old Woman	Wait for how long?
Traveller	Five minutes, that's all.
Narrator 4	So they waited and while they were waiting
Narrator 5	the old woman began to get excited by the thought of the soup
Narrator 8	and she started to talk.
Old Woman	Shall I put another log on the fire?
Traveller	Only if you want to. I don't want to be any trouble.
Narrator 6	So she put another log on the fire
Narrator 7	and the room began to get warmer …
Old Woman	Is the soup ready yet?
Traveller	Let me taste it and I'll tell you.

Woman gives him spoon, he tastes the soup.

Narrator 1	So the man tasted the soup.
Old Woman	Well, what do you think? Is that good?
Traveller	It's very good, but it could be even better with just a little salt and pepper.
Old Woman	Of course.
Narrator 2	So the old woman went to the cupboard
Narrator 3	and gave the man some salt and pepper
Narrator 4	which he added to the pot.
Old Woman	Is that good? (*he tastes it again*)
Traveller	It's very, very good! But it could be even better with just a carrot.

Old Woman	I've got a carrot! I'll fetch it.
Narrator 5	So the old woman went back to the cupboard and came back with a carrot.
Narrator 8	She chopped it into pieces and gave it to the man
Narrator 6	who added it to the pot.
Narrator 7	By now the old woman had forgotten that she was grumpy –
Narrator 1	she even gave the man
Narrators 1–8	a smile!
Old Woman	Tell me, stranger, what's your name?
Traveller	My name's Michael.
Old Woman	And tell me, Michael, is the soup ready yet?
Traveller	It must be. Let me taste it again. (*he tastes it*) Oh, yes, that's wonderful! But it would be the most delicious soup in the world if only …
Old Woman	What?
Traveller	… we had a little meat.
Old Woman	Meat? I have some meat.
Narrator 3	So the old woman went to the cupboard and came back with some meat
Narrator 4	which she cut into pieces and gave to the man
Narrator 5	who added it to the pot.
Old Woman	I can't wait to taste this soup!
Traveller	You must be patient.
Old Woman	I can't. I'm so excited! When will it be ready?
Traveller	Soon. Very, very soon. But I know what will help you wait …
Old Woman	What's that?
Traveller	I'll sing you a song.
Narrator 8	So the man sang the old woman a song
Narrator 6	and it made the old woman feel young again
Narrator 7	and before she knew it, sshh, the man tasted the soup again and said …
Traveller	It's ready!
Old Woman	You fetch some bowls, and I'll fetch us a fine loaf of bread and some wonderful apple juice.
Narrator 1	So they sat down together.
Narrator 2	They ate the soup, they sang more songs.
Narrator 3	They laughed and laughed and laughed, and when the meal was over the old woman gave the man a blanket and let him sleep by the fire while she went to

	bed happier than she had ever been.
NARRATOR 4	But before the man settled down for the night
NARRATOR 5	he went back to the fire, reached into the pot
NARRATOR 8	and said:
TRAVELLER	(*to audience*) And that, my friends, is how you make the most delicious soup in the world from just (*holds up nail*) a rusty old nail!
ALL	Sshhh!
TRAVELLER	(*whispers*) Sorry!

Medium-length plays

17 The Children and the Wind

A humorous play in 12 scenes, based on a fable

Roles	8
Runtime	At least 20 minutes, depending on production
Sets	Billy's home, outside the flour mill; the top of Mighty Mountain; outside and inside Farmer's cottage (split scene). Each change of location in this play is announced as part of the narration and so you have the option of performing without any set whatsoever and letting the audience's imagination do all the hard work!
Props	Stuffed rubber washing-up glove to look like a chicken's comb; a little beak on elastic; something to make a 'nest' from; a box; a few pancakes (could be made of thicker cloth in the right colour); a golden egg (could be a plastic egg painted a golden colour); a 'hitting stick' to be made of something light but rigid (polystyrene perhaps wrapped in cloth painted to look like wood or a cane wrapped in foam rubber and painted)
Style	A light comedy sketch. The main moral lesson conveyed through the play is that dishonesty doesn't pay.
Synopsis	Emily, Hannah and Billy live with their mother in a little hut. One day, the mother wants to make pancakes for her children, but there's no flour at home. The children go to the miller to get some flour, but on the way home the wind blows it away. Hannah goes to the top of the mountain to complain to the wind. He says he can't give her the flour back, but he offers her a magic pancake box instead. The box can produce as many pancakes as they wish, and Hannah is very happy about it. On the way home to the hut she stays overnight with a farmer and his wife. The next day she discovers that the magic box is gone. The same happens a few days later with a magic chicken that the wind gives to Emily instead of the pancake box – a chicken that can lay golden eggs. The girls think the wind has played a trick on them, but Billy knows better. He goes back to see the wind, and this time the wind gives him a magic hitting stick. When Billy stops at the farmer's house, the problem gets solved.
Language level	Intermediate – B1
Language areas	Making requests (*Can you make some …?*); Exclamations (*Don't be silly/greedy, What kind people!*)
Stage tips	Most of the characters have fairly short parts. The farmer and his wife's parts are longer, but some of it is repeated lines. You may want to select the more able students in your class for those roles.

Puchta/Gerngross/Devitt | Get on Stage! | © Helbling Languages

Medium-length plays

The Narrator Chicken has a lot to say too. If you want to make this easier for your students, you can let that character read from a story book. Alternatively, the part of the chicken could be shared between two or three actors.

Materials

Photocopiable Worksheet A p 208
- Comprehension check
- Vocabulary: adjectives
- Polite phrases

Photocopiable Worksheet B p 209
- Phrasal verbs
- *be allowed to* or *let*
- Creative writing: winning the lottery

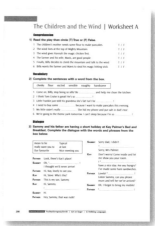

Medium-length plays

The Children and the Wind

Roles Narrator (who is a chicken)   Mother
Hannah   Mavis
Emily   Farmer
Billy   Wind/Prince

Scene 1 Billy's home

Enter Chicken.

CHICKEN (*to audience*) Cluck, cluck, cluck!
Cluck, cluck, cluck!
I'm a chicken not a duck
A duck, you see, says quack, quack, quack
An owl says too-whit, too-whoo –
But I'm a magic chicken
With a story just for you!
Long ago, in a time before supermarkets, there lived three children …
… Hannah:

Enter Hannah.

HANNAH Hello everyone!

CHICKEN … and Emily:

Enter Emily.

EMILY Hello everyone!

CHICKEN … and Billy:

Enter Billy.

BILLY Goodbye, everyone!

ALL Don't be silly, Billy.

CHICKEN Billy, you see, likes being silly sometimes.

BILLY That's not true! I like being silly all the time – but then I get into trouble!

CHICKEN (*to Billy*) Well, can you be sensible for the story?

BILLY I'll try. (*he puts on a 'serious face'*)

CHICKEN Good! Then we'll begin.

Exit Hannah, Billy, Emily. Chicken goes to the side of the stage and settles on her nest.

CHICKEN Hannah, Emily and Billy lived with their mother in a little cottage. Sadly, their father had died some years earlier.

Enter Hannah, Billy, Emily and Mother.

Medium-length plays

HANNAH   Mother, can you make some pancakes, please?

MOTHER   OK, but I haven't got any flour, so you must get me some.

EMILY   OK, Mum. Where can we get some flour?

MOTHER   Go to the miller. He can give you some. Here, take this bowl.

She hands Billy a bowl, which he puts on his head.

BILLY   What a lovely hat! Thank you, Mum.

ALL   Don't be silly, Billy!

BILLY   (*taking off bowl*) Sorry, I forgot.

MOTHER   Off you go.

Exit Hannah, Billy, Emily, Mother.

CHICKEN   And off they went to the miller, where they filled their bowl with flour. They were very happy, but as they walked back, dreaming of pancakes, something happened.

Scene 2   Outside the flour mill

Enter the three children. Billy is holding the bowlful of flour.

HANNAH   What's that noise?

EMILY   I can't hear anything.

BILLY   No, nor can I.

HANNAH   Sshhhh! Just listen.

We hear a whooshing sound made (offstage) by the actor playing Wind.

EMILY   Oh yes! What is that noise?

BILLY   It's my hungry stomach.

HANNAH   Don't be silly, Billy. I think it's the wind.

As she says that line, Wind rushes in and runs about. The students act being blown about.

WIND   It's me, the wind! Hurrah, hurray!
           Don't you love a windy day?
           Fly your kite! Sail your boat!

EMILY   (*shivering*) I wish I had a warmer coat!

WIND	I'm in a rush – I always am – But I'll be back sometime!
	Now, one more blow before I go …
	Wind takes the bowl and blows/tips the flour all over Billy, or if that's too messy just mime the action. Billy sneezes.
	… get your washing on the line!
	Exit Wind.
CHICKEN	And with that, the wind hurried off to blow some people's hats off, and the children went home.

Scene 3 Billy's home

HANNAH	Sorry, Mum, there's no flour.
MOTHER	Why? What happened?
EMILY	The wind blew it all away.
BILLY	I think there's a little bit left in my ears, but not enough for pancakes.
MOTHER	Then you must go and tell the wind to give it back.
HANNAH	I'll go, Mother. Where does the wind live?
MOTHER	At the very top of Mighty Mountain.
EMILY	That's a long way away.
HANNAH	Don't worry – I'm strong!
MOTHER	Be careful, Hannah.
HANNAH	I will be, Mum.
BILLY	A mountain? Here, you might need this. (*hands her a mask and snorkel*)
ALL	Don't be silly, Billy!
CHICKEN	And so brave Hannah climbed the mountain. It took all day, but at last she reached the top.

Scene 4 The top of Mighty Mountain

HANNAH	Wind! Wind! Where are you?
	Enter Wind.
WIND	Here I am! I was just having a rest after all my blowing today.
HANNAH	Yes – well you blew all our flour away, so now we can't have any pancakes.
WIND	No pancakes! Oh, I'm so sorry! I get a bit too excited sometimes and do bad things – but I don't mean to.
HANNAH	I know you don't – my brother Billy's the same – but can we have our flour back, please?

Medium-length plays

WIND   Sorry, I don't have your flour – but I can give you this magic pancake box!

Wind produces a box.

HANNAH   Magic pancake box? (*opens it*) This box is empty! What does it do?

WIND   Well, you just wish for pancakes and when you open it the pancakes will be there. Try it!

Hannah shuts the box.

HANNAH   I wish for pancakes. (*opens the box, and pancakes are inside*) Pancakes!

WIND   Yes.

HANNAH   Oh, thank you, Wind! Now we can have pancakes every day!

CHICKEN   So Hannah started her journey home, but by the time she reached the bottom of the mountain it was starting to get dark. She saw a farmhouse and knocked on the door. The farmer's wife, Mavis, answered.

Scene 5   Farmer's cottage

MAVIS   Yes? What do you want?

HANNAH   I'm so tired and far from home – can I sleep here tonight?

FARMER   Who is it, Mavis?

MAVIS   A young girl. (*imitating Hannah's voice*) She's so tired and far from home – can she sleep here tonight?

FARMER   Has she got any money?

MAVIS   (*imitating Farmer's voice*) Have you got any money?

HANNAH   No, sorry.

MAVIS   (*imitating Hannah's voice again*) No, sorry.

FARMER   (*frowning*) Young people today! Cheeky devils! Go away, go away, go away!

HANNAH   Please – I haven't got any money, but I can pay you with pancakes.

FARMER & MAVIS   (*looking at each other, excited*) Pancakes? Our favourite! (*smiling sweetly*) Come in, come in, come in!

HANNAH   Let me show you my magic pancake box.

FARMER & MAVIS   Magic pancake box?!

Farmer and Mavis grab the box greedily.

FARMER   It's empty!

MAVIS   Get out, get out, get out!

HANNAH   Wait! First, I must say the magic words. 'I wish for pancakes'. Now look!

Farmer and Mavis open the box and see the pancakes.

FARMER   Pancakes, Mavis. Lovely pancakes!

MAVIS   Yes. Let's eat them all.

FARMER	No! Why not wait till morning? Have them for breakfast.
MAVIS	What??!! Wait till morning? Are you mad?
FARMER	(*whispering to Mavis, who seems pleased*) Don't worry, Mavis. I've got an idea. (*then aloud to Hannah*) You can sleep here in the warm kitchen, my dear.
HANNAH	Thank you, sir. You're very kind!
FARMER	Say goodnight, Mavis.
MAVIS	(*still transfixed by the box*) Goodnight, Mavis! … I mean goodnight, young lady.

Farmer drags Mavis away. Hannah settles down.

CHICKEN	And so Hannah fell asleep in front of the fire, dreaming of how happy her family would be when they saw the magic pancake box. But in the night …

Farmer and Mavis creep back in on tiptoe carrying a box that looks the same as Hannah's. The actors can have fun here, 'sshhing' each other, pretending there's a creaky floorboard, pretending to tread on a nail and having to silently scream, pretending one of them suddenly needs the toilet but the other says to wait – whatever they want – but eventually they swap the two boxes and leave.

CHICKEN	Then, in the morning, Cock-a-doodle-doo! (*like a cockerel crowing*)
HANNAH	(*waking and stretching*) What a good night's sleep! Ah, time for pancakes. 'I wish …'
FARMER	(*running in*).Wait!! Don't do that!
HANNAH	But …
MAVIS	(*entering with a plate of pancakes*) Good morning, my dear. I've already taken some pancakes from the box, so don't you worry.
HANNAH	Oh, OK. Thank you. But I think I will go now, if you don't mind, and have breakfast with my family when I get home.
FARMER	(*relieved, bundling her out of the door with the wrong box*) No, of course we don't mind!
MAVIS	Goodbye, my dear. Nice meeting you. Don't call again … I mean, DO call again!
HANNAH	(*a bit confused*) Goodbye, and thank you.
CHICKEN	It was a lovely sunny day, and soon Hannah was back at home where her family were very happy to see her. She told them her amazing story.

Scene 6 Billy's home

HANNAH	(*showing the box*) … and this is the magic pancake box!
BILLY	Go on then, Hannah, say the magic words. I want 20 pancakes.
MOTHER	Don't be greedy, Billy!
HANNAH	OK. I wish for some pancakes. Open the box, Emily!

Emily opens the box.

Medium-length plays

EMILY	It's empty!
HANNAH	What? Impossible!
MOTHER	Oh, poor Hannah – the wind's played a trick on you.
BILLY	Maybe we can eat the box.
ALL	Don't be silly, Billy!
HANNAH	Sorry, everyone.
EMILY	Don't worry, Hannah. I'll go and ask the wind for our flour.
MOTHER	Oh, be careful, Emily.
EMILY	Don't worry, Mum. I will.
CHICKEN	And so brave Emily climbed the mountain. It took all day, but at last she reached the top.

Scene 7   **The top of Mighty Mountain**

EMILY   Wind! Wind! Where are you?

Enter Wind.

WIND   Here I am! I was just going out to blow some clouds across the sky.

EMILY   Yes, well, you blew all our flour away yesterday and now we can't have any pancakes.

WIND   No pancakes! Oh, I'm so sorry! I get a bit too excited sometimes and do bad things, but I don't mean to.

EMILY   I know you don't – my brother Billy's the same – but can we have our flour back, please?

WIND   Sorry, I don't have your flour, but I can give you this magic chicken. (*indicates Chicken, who is sitting on her nest, dreamily watching the play*)

Nothing happens.

WIND   (*a bit louder*) This magic chicken.

Still nothing happens.

WIND   Oi! That's you!

The Chicken realises and joins in.

CHICKEN   (*to audience*) It's me! (*to other characters*) Sorry, carry on.

EMILY   Magic chicken? What does she do?

WIND	Well, you just wish for gold. The magic chicken will cluck three times and then lay a golden egg. You can sell the egg and buy lots of pancakes. Try it!

Emily stands next to the Chicken.

EMILY	I wish for gold.
CHICKEN	Cluck, cluck, cluck!

She crouches down, a bit of straining, someone does a descending whistle and a pop! sound by flicking their finger out from inside their cheek. When she stands up, there is a golden egg (which the actor has hidden in their hand up to that point, or whatever clever plan the actors may have devised).

EMILY	A golden egg!
WIND	Yes.
EMILY	Oh, thank you, Wind. Now we can have pancakes every day!
CHICKEN	So Emily started her journey home, but by the time she reached the bottom of the mountain it was starting to get dark. She saw a farmhouse and knocked on the door. Mavis answered.

Scene 8 Farmer's cottage

MAVIS	Yes? What do you want? Can't you see I'm busy? I'm eating pancakes.
EMILY	I'm so tired and far from home – can I sleep here tonight?
FARMER	Who is it, Mavis?
MAVIS	A young girl. (*imitating Emily's voice*) She's so tired and far from home – can she sleep here tonight?
FARMER	Has she got any money?
MAVIS	(*imitating the Farmer's voice*) Have you got any money?
EMILY	No, sorry.
MAVIS	(*imitating Emily's voice again*) No, sorry.
FARMER	(*frowning*) Young people today – cheeky devils! Go away, go away, go away!
EMILY	Please. I haven't got any money, but I can pay you with gold.
FARMER & MAVIS	(*looking at each other, excited*) Gold! Our favourite! (*smiling sweetly*) Come in, come in, come in!

Emily enters, followed by Chicken.

FARMER	Wait a minute! Chickens aren't allowed in the house!
EMILY	This is my magic chicken.
FARMER & MAVIS	Magic chicken?!
FARMER	But this is just a boring ordinary chicken!
CHICKEN	How dare you!
MAVIS	Get out, get out, get out!

Medium-length plays

EMILY　　Wait! I must say the magic words. 'I wish for gold'. Now look!

Chicken repeats the actions from before, with the same sound effects, and a golden egg is produced.

FARMER　　Gold, Mavis! Lovely gold!

MAVIS　　Yes. Give it to me. GIMME!!

FARMER　　No, Mavis. The gold belongs to this young lady.

MAVIS　　What??!! What are you saying? Are you mad? It's gold!!!

FARMER　　(*whispering to Mavis, who seems pleased*) Don't worry, Mavis. I've got an idea. (*aloud to Emily*) You can sleep here in the warm kitchen, my dear.

EMILY　　Thank you, sir. You're very kind. But please take the gold, I want to pay you.

FARMER　　No, I don't want the gold – you keep it! Say goodnight, Mavis.

MAVIS　　(*still transfixed by the golden egg*) Goodnight, Mavis! … I mean goodnight, young lady.

Farmer drags Mavis away. Emily settles down, with Chicken lying beside her.

EMILY　　What kind people!

CHICKEN　　And so Emily fell asleep in front of the fire, dreaming of how happy her family would be when they saw me, the magic chicken. I fell asleep too, but in the night …

Farmer and Mavis creep back in on tiptoe. The chicken starts to wake up and cluck. The farmer and Mavis panic. Mavis tries to put her hand over the chicken's beak but the chicken pecks it hard, and Mavis silently screams. Then the farmer takes off his sock and waves it in front of the chicken, and the terrible smell makes the chicken faint, so they can wrestle it offstage. Once they're out of sight of the audience, a scarf is tied around the chicken's neck as fast as possible, and they all re-enter, pretending it's an entirely different chicken. (The audience will know it's the same chicken actor, just with a scarf on, but that's all part of the fun.) Emily stirs a little through all this, but does not wake up.

FARMER　　(*whispering to 'wrong' chicken*). Right you! You sleep here.

Chicken lies down beside Emily, in the same place as the magic chicken.

MAVIS　　(*whispering to Farmer*). Come on! Let's lock the magic chicken away in the hen house.

Farmer and Mavis sneak off again, but not before Mavis has stolen the golden egg.

CHICKEN　　(*maybe in a different voice/accent*) Well, what a treat! Those old fools never let me sleep in the house. At last, a good night's sleep safe from the fox. It's so warm I won't need my scarf. (*takes it off*).

Chicken settles down but just as she is about to fall asleep we hear (offstage) Cock-a-doodle-doo!

Medium-length plays

CHICKEN	I don't believe it! Typical!
EMILY	(*waking and stretching*). Good morning, Chicken! What a good night's sleep. I really want to pay the farmer and his wife for their kindness. Now where's that golden egg? ... (*searches around*) How strange – it's gone! Ah well, never mind, I'll just get another one. (*goes to the chicken*). I wish for ...
FARMER	(*running in*) Wait!! Don't do that!
EMILY	Why not? I want to pay you for your kindness. I wish for a g ...
FARMER	Stop! Pleeeeeease don't!
EMILY	Why not?
MAVIS	(*entering in a panic*) Because I was up early this morning and took the egg to ... um ...
FARMER	Polish it for you!
MAVIS	That's right! To polish it for you! (*picks up the chicken's scarf and polishes the egg*)
EMILY	I see. You are so kind! Please keep the egg. I really want you to.
FARMER	Well, if it makes you happy.
EMILY	Yes, if you keep the egg I'll be really happy.
MAVIS	Then we will keep the egg. Thank you!
EMILY	I'll go now, if you don't mind.
FARMER	(*relieved, bundling her out of the door with the wrong chicken*) No, of course we don't mind!
MAVIS	Goodbye, my dear. Nice meeting you. Don't call again ... I mean, DO call again.
EMILY	(*a bit confused*) Goodbye, and thank you!
CHICKEN	It was a lovely sunny day, and soon Emily was back at home where her family were very happy to see her. She told them her amazing story.

Scene 9 Billy's home

EMILY	... and this is the magic chicken.
CHICKEN	Eh?
BILLY	Go on then, Emily, say the magic words. I want to be so rich I can have a servant to blow my nose for me!
MOTHER	Don't be silly, Billy.
EMILY	OK – I wish for gold!
CHICKEN	Sorry?
EMILY	I said, 'I wish for gold!'
CHICKEN	Why are you telling me that?
HANNAH	Because you're a magic chicken, and Emily says you lay golden eggs.
EMILY	That's right. I saw you do it!

Medium-length plays

CHICKEN What? Impossible. I'm just an ordinary chicken. (*to audience*) Well, I suppose a talking chicken isn't exactly ordinary.

MOTHER Oh, poor Emily. The wind has played a trick on you like it did on Hannah.

EMILY Sorry, everyone.

BILLY Wait a minute. I think I know what's happened. I'll go and ask the wind for our flour. But I don't think it's the wind that's been naughty.

MOTHER Oh, be careful, Billy.

BILLY Don't worry, Mum. I will.

CHICKEN And so brave but silly Billy climbed the mountain. It took all day, but at last he reached the top.

Scene 10   The top of Mighty Mountain

BILLY Wind! Wind! Where are you?

Enter Wind.

WIND Here I am! I was just going out to blow bonfire smoke into people's eyes.

BILLY Yes … well, the day before yesterday you blew all our flour away and now we can't have any pancakes.

WIND No pancakes! Oh! I'm so sorry. I get a bit too excited sometimes and do bad things, but I don't mean to.

BILLY I know you don't, because I'm the same.

WIND I'm sorry I can't give you your flour back. All I have is this magic hitting stick.

BILLY Magic hitting stick? How does it work?

WIND You say 'Hit, stick, hit!' and the stick will beat anyone who deserves to be beaten.

BILLY Can I try it?

WIND Don't be silly, Billy – it won't work! It won't beat people who are good, and I know you're good.

BILLY May I have the stick anyhow?

WIND Of course, but it won't get you any pancakes.

BILLY Wrong, my friend! I think it's exactly what I need to get some pancakes. Goodbye, Wind.

CHICKEN Billy started his journey home, and by the time he reached the bottom of the mountain it was starting to get dark. He saw the farmhouse and knocked on the door. Mavis answered.

Medium-length plays

Scene 11 **Farmer's cottage**

MAVIS
: Yes? What do you want? Can't you see I'm busy? I'm eating pancakes and counting gold.

BILLY
: (*whispers to audience*) Aha! Just as I thought. (*aloud to Mavis*) I'm so tired and far from home – can I sleep here tonight?

FARMER
: Who is it, Mavis?

MAVIS
: A young man. (*imitating Billy's voice*) He's so tired and far from home – can he sleep here tonight?

FARMER
: I don't need pancakes and I don't need gold, so tell him to go away.

MAVIS
: (*imitating farmer's voice*) He doesn't need pancakes and he doesn't need gold, so go away, go away, go away!

BILLY
: Listen, please! With all that gold, aren't you afraid of robbers?

FARMER & MAVIS
: Robbers! What do you mean?

BILLY
: If robbers hear about your gold they'll come and steal it from you – and maybe they'll steal everything else as well!

FARMER
: Oh no! I didn't think about that.

MAVIS
: I'm scared! What can we do?

BILLY
: Well, if you let me sleep in your lovely warm kitchen I'll tell you about my magic hitting stick.

FARMER & MAVIS
: Magic hitting stick!?

BILLY
: Yes! If you say 'Hit, stick, hit', it'll beat your enemies black and blue!

FARMER
: (*to Mavis*) That would keep the robbers away.

MAVIS
: Yes it would! (*to Billy*) Show us how it works!

FARMER
: Not now, Mavis. The young man's tired. Come in, come in, come in, and sleep by the fire. We can talk in the morning.

MAVIS
: What? What are you saying? I can't wait until then! I want to … (*but the farmer just looks at her and she realises he has another cunning plan*).
Oh, I see! Yes, tomorrow will be fine. We can talk, and eat pancakes.

FARMER
: That's right, my dear. That's right. Now say goodnight, Mavis.

MAVIS
: Goodnight, Mavis! … I mean, goodnight, young man.

They exit yawning and stretching, pretending they are tired. Billy puts the stick down.

CHICKEN
: The greedy farmer and his wife pretended to go to bed and Billy lay down – but he only pretended to go to sleep, because Billy wasn't as silly as everyone thought.

Billy does some pretend snoring.

CHICKEN
: And later that night …

Medium-length plays

Chicken sleeps ... again, the farmer and Mavis creep in with lots of 'sshhing' and pointing and silliness, which the actors can invent. They have a stick identical to Billy's. Billy has one eye open, but every time they look at him he closes it. Eventually they find the magic stick, swap it and silently celebrate, waving it about but then ...

BILLY (*sitting up*) Hit, stick, hit!

The stick then starts to whack the farmer and Mavis. Of course the actors do this themselves, pretending that the stick has a life of its own. The farmer whacks himself and calls for help; Mavis helps, and they both wrestle with the stick for a bit as it whacks them both; then Mavis gets the stick and it whacks her, and so on. This section must be safe but it must be very, very silly and energetic and noisy. If the stick is made of something light but rigid (polystyrene perhaps wrapped in cloth painted to look like wood or a cane wrapped in foam rubber and painted), then the actors can go wild whilst not putting themselves in any danger. Eventually ...

FARMER Please make it stop!

MAVIS Yes, please make it stop!

BILLY You must be robbers! The stick will only stop when you promise to give back the things you've stolen. Do you promise?

FARMER Yes, we promise, we promise! Please make it stop!

BILLY Say it, then.

MAVIS We promise to give back the magic pancake box.

FARMER And the magic chicken.

BILLY Good. Stop, stick, stop!

The stick stops, and the farmer and Mavis collapse. Billy retrieves the stick.

CHICKEN And so everything ended happily. The magic pancake box was returned to its owners.

Scene 12 **Billy's home**

Hannah enters with the magic pancake box full of pancakes.

HANNAH Look everyone! Pancakes at last!

CHICKEN And the magic chicken – that's me! – was returned to its owners.

Emily enters and puts her arm around the chicken. She clucks three times – usual sound effects – and Emily holds up a golden egg (which she has brought on stage behind her back but pretends to get from the chicken's rear end). Or Emily just brings a basket of golden eggs on with her.

EMILY Look everyone. Gold! We're rich.

CHICKEN And Billy still has the magic hitting stick.

FARMER	(*waking up*) What? Oh no! Run, Mavis, run!
MAVIS	Aaarrrghhh! Mummy!
	They run off.
CHICKEN	And Mother married a handsome prince.
ALL	What??!!!!
MOTHER	(*entering*) Did I?
CHICKEN	Not really, but this is a fairy tale and we must all live happily ever after.
MOTHER	I'm as happy as I can be with my children safely back at home.
HANNAH	Oh, but Mother it would be lovely if you married a handsome prince.
	All make the sound of a trumpet fanfare. A handsome prince enters magnificently, except it's the same actor who played the Wind, wearing a crown.
PRINCE	Did someone call? (*sees Mother, runs to her and goes down on one knee*) My darling, will you marry me?
ALL	Hurray!
PRINCE	(*to Billy*) Tell me, Billy, how does that magic hitting stick work?
BILLY	Well you say the magic words 'Hit, stick …' (*he stops abruptly*) Sorry, I can't tell you.
ALL	Why not?
BILLY	(*points at audience*) There may be robbers here!
ALL	THE END!

Medium-length plays

18 The Wise Judge

A funny one-scene play based on a traditional story

Roles 3

Runtime Around 4 minutes, depending on production

Set In the woods

Props Trees and bushes painted onto a big piece of cardboard or big sheets of paper and fixed onto the wall as a backdrop. An axe (made of a stick and cardboard) and a saw (cardboard) would be good to have but are not absolutely necessary. Students holding a few leafy twigs could act as the trees that the woodcutter is chopping down.

Style Traditional story

Synopsis A woodcutter is cutting down trees for the judge. He is glad when a farmer offers his help, but to his surprise he realises that all the farmer is doing is watching him do his hard work and grunting whenever he swings the axe. The woodcutter is even more surprised when the farmer asks him to pay him because he has 'helped' him with his work by grunting. The woodcutter decides to see the judge about their disagreement. The judge says that indeed the farmer has a right to be paid, and the farmer is delighted to hear that. The judge takes a bagful of money and shakes it. He asks the farmer if he can hear the sound that the coins make. When the farmer confirms that, the judge says that he has been paid as 'the sound of money is the right pay for the sound of work'.

Language level Elementary – A2

Language areas Present continuous (*What are you doing? I'm cutting wood. My friend the judge is building a house etc.*)

Stage tips Given that this is a very short play it may be fun to perform without a single prop or piece of scenery and encourage students who aren't playing the three characters to create the sounds of the forest, the sounds of a tree being chopped, the sound of a mighty tree falling, the sound of coins clinking in a bag, whatever they feel would be entertaining and that involves having discussed it among themselves. Let them surprise you! Mime the axe, mime the money bag and improvise ideas to help make these mimed images clear in terms of story-telling.

Medium-length plays

Materials Photocopiable Worksheet p 210
- Comprehension check
- Vocabulary: exclamations
- Present continuous

Medium-length plays

The Wise Judge

Roles Woodcutter
Farmer
Judge

A man is chopping down a tree in the woods. After a few hefty blows he stands back and looks up.

WOODCUTTER (*shouts*) Timberrrrrr!

He mimes watching the mighty tree crash to the forest floor. Satisfied, he then starts on another tree, when another man appears and sits down nearby.

FARMER Good afternoon.

WOODCUTTER Good afternoon.

FARMER What are you doing?

WOODCUTTER Can't you see? Cutting trees down!

FARMER Why are you cutting trees down?

WOODCUTTER My good friend the judge is building a new house and I need to chop 20 trees down for him by the end of the day.

FARMER Ahhhh – you must be very tired.

WOODCUTTER I am, and he's coming to pay me at 5 o'clock – but I've still got one more tree to chop down.

FARMER But it's 4.50 now! Shall I help you?

WOODCUTTER That would be good. There's another axe over there.

FARMER Oh, I won't help you like that.

WOODCUTTER Then how?

FARMER Just chop and see!

The woodcutter continues chopping. Every time he swings his axe the farmer lets out a loud grunt.

WOODCUTTER What are you doing?

FARMER Helping!

WOODCUTTER You're bonkers! That's no help!

He continues to chop, and each chop is accompanied by the farmer making his strange noises. After a few chops the woodcutter stands back, looks up and shouts ...

WOODCUTTER Timberrrrrr!

As they both mime watching the tree fall, the farmer creaks like a tree trunk splitting, and as the tree 'hits the forest floor' he goes 'Crash!'

WOODCUTTER	Can you help me saw off the branches?
FARMER	Give me my money first!
WOODCUTTER	Money? What for?
FARMER	For my help.
WOODCUTTER	For your help? You didn't do anything!
FARMER	Well I grunted for you, didn't I?
WOODCUTTER	You're crazy! Nobody pays for grunting.
FARMER	Let's see what the judge says.
WOODCUTTER	OK, let's see what he says. Here he comes now.

Enter Judge.

JUDGE	Hello, Farmer Giles. What brings you here?
FARMER	I helped this man when he was cutting down trees, and he doesn't want to pay me for my help.
JUDGE	I see. (*turning to the woodcutter*) Is that true?
WOODCUTTER	It's true I was chopping wood.
JUDGE	(*to farmer*) And what did he do?
WOODCUTTER	He grunted.
JUDGE	Is that true?
FARMER	Yes, I helped him by grunting.
JUDGE	(*to woodcutter*) OK. I've got your money here (*shows them a bag which he shakes and we hear the clink of coins*) and I think Farmer Giles does need payment for the help he gave you.
WOODCUTTER	What???
FARMER	(*rubbing his hands greedily*) Haha! Yes, yes – give me the money!
WOODCUTTER	But that's not fair, sir!

JUDGE	Please just wait. (*to Farmer*) Come here, Farmer Giles.

Farmer Giles steps up to him, getting more and more excited. The Judge shakes the bag again a few times.

JUDGE	(*to farmer*) Can you hear the sound of the coins?
FARMER	(*jumping up and down and holding his hands up*) Yes I can, yes I can!
JUDGE	Then you've been paid. The sound of money is the proper pay for the sound of working (*he turns and hands the bag to the woodcutter*) – and money is the proper pay for work!

Chapter 4
Teenage dramas

Teenage dramas

19 Good Girl

A teenage drama in 6 scenes

Roles	7–14 (doubling of roles recommended); if possible, a few extra students for non-speaking parts in Scene 3
Runtime	Around 14 minutes, depending on production
Sets	The school drama club; Ruby's home; the street by a box office; a split scene – the school drama club/Ruby's room
Props	Scripts; Dad's diary; money and tickets (can be made by the students); Goth outfit; black-and-white face paint
Style	Modern drama
Synopsis	The play shows how teenage Ruby gets ignored by her family, her teachers and complete strangers. When her drama teacher chooses the different parts in *King Arthur*, she gets the role of a servant without any lines to speak, although her teacher had promised she would get a better part this time. It turns out her parents have forgotten about the performance and can't come to see it because they haven't got time. When Ruby gets asked to give her concert tickets to someone else she does so.
	Finally Ruby decides she's had enough of her feelings being ignored all the time, and everyone expecting her to be the 'understanding' person. She's determined to do something in order to get noticed by people. And so she does, and shocks teachers and family by turning Goth. Her parents suffer deeply from what they think the neighbours must be saying about Ruby – until one day they find out that their daughter is very popular with the neighbours, as she helps them a lot. Ruby's parents learn their lesson …
Language level	Intermediate – B1
Language areas	*Will*-future; *going to*-future.
	If-clauses, e.g. *If I do this, people will notice me. If I gave you somebody else's part, they'd be upset. If you had said something, we'd have reacted differently.*
	Want someone to do something, e.g. *I don't want people to assume they can just ignore my feelings all the time.*
	Language chunks with *if*: *It's as if people just didn't notice me. I wonder if the wizard has defeated the evil witch.*
Stage tips	This is one of the longer plays in this collection. If you're concerned with the length of the roles but would like your students to act out this play, we would recommend doubling the longer roles, especially Ruby's. This can best be done if,

at any point(s) in the play specified by you, the girl acting as Ruby hands over to the girl stepping into the role an easily recognisable piece of costume that clearly shows who is playing Ruby. It can be quite cool theatrically to see a part being handed over mid-play by, for instance, a lime green bomber jacket being taken off by one actress who then puts it onto another actress thus visibly 'handing over' the part.

Another option would be to leave out Scene 3 completely. This means, however, that you would lose 4 characters: Customer, Assistant, Boy and Man which provide opportunities for other students to act in the play in smaller, less challenging, roles.

Important! – Should you decide to cut Scene 3 altogether, Ruby's monologue in Scene 4 would need to be changed, as follows:

'Right – that's enough! First my drama teacher (*mocking*) 'Sorry, but it's too late now. If I gave you somebody else's part, they'd be upset. You *do* understand, don't you?' Then Mum and Dad. Who never have time for me. (*mockingly*) 'You *do* understand, don't you, sweetheart?' But I don't *want* to be everybody's good girl any more. I don't *want* people to assume they can just ignore my feelings all the time. I don't *want* to be the understanding one. It's almost like people are just ignoring me, as if I wasn't really there. As if people just didn't notice me! (*she starts leafing through the magazine*) As if people just didn't *notice* me!

Ah, that's it! (*she bangs her fist on the magazine*). I've got an idea. If I do it, people WILL NOTICE ME!'

Materials **Photocopiable Worksheet A p 211**

- Comprehension check
- Vocabulary
- *if*-clauses

Photocopiable Worksheet B p 212

- 2nd conditional
- *if*-clauses
- Creative writing: a poster

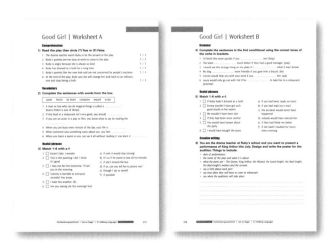

Teenage dramas

Good Girl

Roles Mr Phillips, the drama teacher   Ruby's dad
Jack   Ruby's mum
Olivia   Mrs Carter (neighbour)
Charlie   Box office assistant
Amy   Customer
Tom   Boy
Ruby   Boy's dad

Scene 1 The school drama club

Mr Phillips OK, kids, listen up. For our end of the year play, we'll do a performance of *King Arthur* this year.

Charlie *King Arthur*, cool!

Jack Can I be the king, sir?

Tom And I'd like to be …

Mr Phillips Well, listen … I've already chosen who'll play the different parts. I think it'll work better that way.

Kids All right. So who's going to be who?

Mr Phillips Well, listen … Tom, you'll be King Arthur. (*hands Tom the script*)

Tom Thank you, sir!

Mr Phillips Olivia, you'll be the queen. (*hands Olivia the script*)

Olivia The queen? Great! Thanks.

Mr Phillips Charlie, you'll be the wizard. (*hands Charlie the script*)

Charlie OK. Do I get a wand, sir?

Mr Phillips Of course.

Jack, you'll be the good knight. (*hands Jack the script*)

Jack OK.

Mr Phillips You, James, will be the bad knight. (*hands James the script*)

James The bad knight, OK.

Mr Phillips And Amy, you'll be the bad knight's mother. She's a witch. (*hands Amy the script*).

James Oh no – my mother's a witch!

Kids Hee hee hee!

Ruby And me?

Mr Phillips Oh, Ruby, of course. I almost forgot. You'll be the servant. (*doesn't hand Ruby a script*)
OK, you've all got your scripts. Read them carefully, and I'll see you on Wednesday. Then we'll go through the script, and we'll do a first read-through. This means you don't need to learn your script by heart, but read it carefully, so you can begin to understand your part. All right everyone?

Teenage dramas

Kids	Sure.
Ruby	Excuse me, sir?
Mr Phillips	Ruby?
Ruby	I didn't get a script.
Mr Phillips	Yeah, you don't need one. You're just the servant. You don't have any lines. In fact, you don't really need to be here on Wednesday. We'll slot you in later. Is that OK?
Ruby	That's fine, sir.
Mr Phillips	So, OK, everyone. See you Wednesday!

Exit kids except Ruby, who stays behind.

Ruby	Sir?
Mr Phillips	What is it, Ruby?
Ruby	Remember last year when we did *Babes in the Wood*?
Mr Phillips	Yeah, it was a fine production, if I say so myself. I don't remember you being in it!
Ruby	I was, but I was only a tree. When will I get a part with lines?
Mr Phillips	Maybe next year.
Ruby	You said that last year, sir.
Mr Phillips	Did I? Sorry, but it's too late now. If I gave you somebody else's part, they'd be upset. You do understand, don't you?
Ruby	Yes, I understand.
Mr Phillips	Good girl!

Exit both.

Scene 2 Ruby's home

Her mum is busy on her computer, and her dad is studying some documents.

Ruby	Hi, Mum! Hi, Dad!

No answer.

Ruby	What's that burning smell, Mum?
Mum	Smell? What smell? Oh, that's your dinner, Ruby. It's in the oven. Can you go and get it yourself? We've got very little time. We're going out tonight.
Ruby	You're going out? I didn't know that.
Dad	Didn't we tell you?
Ruby	No, you didn't.
Dad	We must have forgotten, then. We were both so busy, you see.
Mum	Sorry. Anyway, thanks for babysitting your little brother tonight.

Teenage dramas

Ruby Babysitting! But Mum, you know I've got homework to do.

Dad We know, darling. But it's not for tomorrow, is it?

Ruby No, it's not.

Mum That's good. But we've really got to go now, sweetheart.

Ruby One more thing … you do remember, don't you? My play's next week!

Mum Oh, dear. We almost forgot! Derek, get your diary out.

Dad (*fetching his diary and looking at it*). All right, when is it?

Ruby Well, it's on three different days … Monday …

Mum Mmh. I can't. I've got my aerobics class.

Dad And I'm playing tennis.

Ruby … Wednesday …

Dad I'm sure that's a possibility. Let me see. Wednesday? Sorry, I've got a guest for a business dinner.

Mum And I'm going to my slimming club.

Ruby … and Friday!

Mum Friday's no problem, is it Derek? (*consults diary*) Oh, how unfortunate – I'm meeting my friends on Friday.

Dad Yeah, and I'll be in Paris. I won't be back before midnight. Really sorry, darling.

There is a brief but awkward pause. Mum and Dad realise Ruby is disappointed by the fact that they didn't add her play dates to their diaries.

Mum Have you got a big role in the play, Ruby?

Ruby No I haven't. I'm only a servant.

Dad Do you have any lines?

Ruby No, I don't.

Dad Well, then it's not such a problem really, is it? I promise I'll come when you have a real part. You do understand, don't you, sweetheart?

Ruby Yes, I understand.

Mum Good girl!

Scene 3   The street, by a box office

Ruby is queuing up to buy tickets for a concert. One customer is in front of her. There is a father with a young boy behind her. She is talking on the phone.

Ruby Hi Olivia, I'm queuing up for the tickets … yeah, for the concert … no, don't worry … I'm sure I'll get two tickets … no, no, no … there's only one person in front of me. Yeah, sure I'll give you a ring. Bye! (*switches phone off*)

Customer Two tickets for the show on Saturday, please.

Assistant Two tickets for Saturday. That's £36, please.

Teenage dramas

CUSTOMER	Here you are.
ASSISTANT	Thank you. And here are the tickets.
CUSTOMER	Bye.
ASSISTANT	Bye.
RUBY	Two tickets for Saturday, please.
ASSISTANT	You're lucky, young lady; these are the last two tickets, then we're sold out. (*She puts up a SOLD OUT sign.*)
PEOPLE IN QUEUE	Oh, no! (*some start leaving – but the man and boy behind her stay*)
ASSISTANT	That's £36.
RUBY	Here you are. Thanks.
ASSISTANT	Thank you.

Boy behind her starts crying.

BOY	But I wanted to see the show, Dad!
MAN	(*to Ruby*) Look, he was so looking forward to the concert, and now you've got the last two tickets.
RUBY	I'm really sorry. But ...
MAN	It's his birthday treat, I promised him ...
RUBY	I see, but don't worry, the same show's on again in 2 weeks' time.
MAN	Well, that's no good for us. In 2 weeks' time his birthday'll be over.
	But you don't mind selling us the tickets, do you? You can always go in 2 weeks' time, can't you?
RUBY	Ah, OK ... well, I guess I can.
MAN	Right. Here's your money then. (*hands Ruby the money, she hands him the tickets*) That's very kind. You do understand, don't you?
RUBY	Yes, I understand.
MAN	Good girl!

Scene 4 Ruby's room

Some time later: Ruby is sitting in her room, looking at a magazine. She is angry/frustrated, talking to herself.

RUBY Right – that's enough! First my drama teacher (*mocking*) 'Sorry, but it's too late now. If I gave you somebody else's part, they'd be upset. You do understand, don't you?' Then Mum and Dad. Who never have time for me. (*mocking*) 'You do understand, don't you, sweetheart?' And finally I'm stupid enough to hand over to a man and his 7-year-old kid – who I've never met before! – tickets that I got for a concert I've been looking forward to for ages. (*mocking*) 'You do understand, don't you?'
But I don't want to be everybody's good girl any more. I don't want people to assume they can just ignore my feelings all the time. I don't want to be the

Teenage dramas

understanding one. It's almost like people are just ignoring me, as if I wasn't really there. As if people just didn't notice me! (*she starts leafing through the magazine*) As if people just didn't notice me!

Ah, that's it! (*she bangs her fist on the magazine*). I've got an idea. If I do it, people *WILL NOTICE ME!*

Scene 5 **Split scene: school drama club and Ruby's home**

Ruby plays both scenes simultaneously, standing in the middle between the parts of both locations.

Mr Phillips	All right, everyone. Let's get going. Does everyone know their lines?
Kids	Yes, sir.
Mr Phillips	Good. Off we go! The thunder rumbles, the lightning flashes, and …
Witch	(*cackles*) Hahahaha! I've cast the spell and soon the kingdom shall be yours, my son!
Bad knight	Oh Mother, I love you! You're so eeeeevil!
Witch	Thank you, son, I try my best.
Good knight	Not so fast, you two! With my trusty sword I'll defeat you both!
Witch	(*cackles*) You can never defeat me with my powerful magic!

Enter Wizard.

Wizard	No, but with my powerful … erm … finger (*using his finger as he has forgotten his wand*) I'll put a stop to your evil ways!
Mr Phillips	Charlie?
Wizard	Yes, sir?
Mr Phillips	You appear to have forgotten something. Where's your wand?
Wizard	A dog ate it, sir.
Mr Phillips	That's so ridiculous, I think I'll believe you! OK, let's move on to the scene in the king's castle. Tom? Olivia? When you're ready.
Queen	My dear husband, I wonder if the wizard has defeated the evil witch.
King	Patience, dear queen. I'm sure we'll have some good news soon. I'll call a servant to bring us some food and drink. Servant? (*claps his hands, but nothing happens*)
Queen	Servant? (*shouts – nothing happens*)
Mr Phillips	Where's Ruby?
Charlie	She's not here, sir.
Mum	Where's Ruby?
Dad	I don't know. She should be back home by now, shouldn't she?
Mum	Ah, well, she'll be home soon, I'm sure. She's such a *good* girly.
Dad	Yeah, that's right. But I just hope she hasn't forgotten she needs to tidy up the living room for us. My guests'll be here in an hour.

Teenage dramas

Enter Ruby in full Goth style, and stands between the two scenes.

RUBY	Hi!
DAD	Ruby? You must be joking!
RUBY	Joking? Why?
MR PHILLIPS	Because that's not a servant's costume.
RUBY	What makes you think this is a costume, sir?
MUM	Well, just look at yourself!
RUBY	I don't need to. I know what I look like.
DAD	Come on, be a good girl. Take it off – we know you're just joking!
CHARLIE	Good joke actually – hee hee hee!!
RUBY	(*to both sides*) Listen. This is *not* a joke, right! And I'm *not* taking this off, *ever*.
MUM	What? You're not taking it off?
OLIVIA	You mean you want to go to *school* like this?
DAD	And walk around the *neighbourhood* like this?
RUBY	That's right!
DAD	But what …?
RUBY	But what *what*?
MUM	… what will the neighbours say?
TOM	And what will the headmaster say?
RUBY	No idea what they'll say, and I honestly don't care at all.
DAD	Oh, come on, Ruby. Be our good girl. We can't have a daughter who walks around like this!
MR PHILLIPS	We can't have a student who walks around like this!
ALL	You *do* understand, don't you?
RUBY	It's *you* who *don't* understand. I'm not taking this off. This is me, and I don't care what you think. Live with it! (*She walks off, leaving them all speechless.*)

Scene 6   **Ruby's home, five weeks later**

MUM	I just don't understand her any more. These past few weeks have been so difficult.
DAD	Yeah, she was such a good girl.
MUM	Just imagine what the neighbours must be saying about us …
DAD	Don't remind me, please. It's so embarrassing.

Silence, interrupted by the doorbell.

MUM	Who's that?
DAD	I don't know. (*he goes to the window, and peeps out*)

Teenage dramas

DAD Oh, no! It's Mrs Carter from next door. She's probably coming round to complain about Ruby.

MUM Well, let's pretend we're not here, then.

DAD We can't. She's already seen me. (*opens the door*)

DAD Good evening. Do come in, please.

MUM Good evening Mrs Carter. Very nice to see you.

MRS CARTER I'm lucky you're at home, aren't I? You're such busy people!

DAD Well, yes, you know what it's like. Life's pretty hectic.

MRS CARTER I'm here because of your daughter.

DAD Ruby? I knew it! What's the problem?

MRS CARTER Problem? There's no problem. I just wondered whether you could give this to her, please?

MUM To Ruby? Erm … yes … sure. But she's not at home right now …

MRS CARTER Yes, I know. It's Friday evening, isn't it? I know she's never at home on a Friday evening. That's why I called. Anyway, just give it to her, please. I must be off. (*she leaves*)

DAD See? They're all talking about her. (*mocking*) 'I know. It's Friday evening, isn't it? I know she's never at home on a Friday evening!' It's terrible, isn't it?

MUM It is. Poor Mrs Carter came round tonight because she knew Ruby wouldn't be here. She must be terrified of her.

DAD It's the way she looks, isn't it? Awful!

MUM What's in the box, do you think?

DAD Maybe it's soap. So Ruby can wash that ridiculous warpaint off her face!

MUM Listen!

DAD What?

MUM The front door's opening. Must be Ruby.

DAD Let's hide quickly. I want to know what's in the parcel.

Enter Ruby. She sees the parcel and picks it up.

RUBY A parcel. And it's for me! Can't be from Mum and Dad. I'm not their good girl any more. Well, let's see.

She starts unwrapping the present. There's a jumper in it. She takes it out and looks at it. Unnoticed by her, Mum and Dad have entered the room.

RUBY Wow. That's a cool jumper. Who's that from? Oh, there's a letter!

She opens it, and starts reading.

'Dear Ruby, this is a little thank-you present from us all. We are very proud that a young girl like you gives up so much time helping others. We hope you like the jumper! Love, Mrs Carter and your twelve other neighbours in Park Lane.'

Teenage dramas

MUM 'Twelve other neighbours'?

RUBY Oh. Mum – you frightened me! I hadn't noticed you were here. And Dad, you too!

DAD Well, I don't understand. Giving up so much of your time helping others – what's going on here?

RUBY Well, you know Mr and Mrs Jones from the house next door, don't you?

DAD Yeah, why?

RUBY Well, they're both very frail now, and they can't do much work at home …

MUM So?

RUBY So I decided I'd help them a bit. Do some of their housework, and the shopping and things.

DAD Hang on a minute. So … when we think you go out and meet with your Goth friends on Friday evenings, you're …

MUM … helping the Joneses?

RUBY That's right. They're very nice people, Mum. I really like them, and they're so grateful for the help.

DAD That's marvellous! But why didn't you tell us? If you'd said something, we'd have reacted differently.

RUBY I didn't tell you because you're always so busy.

DAD Everybody else in our street knew what you were doing of course …

MUM … yeah, it was only us who didn't notice.

DAD And we were too worried about how you looked and what the neighbours …

MUM … might be thinking of you.

DAD I'm sorry, Ruby.

MUM Me, too.

RUBY That's OK, Mum, Dad. At least I got your attention.

DAD So let me get this right. Because we never listened to you, you became a Goth?

RUBY Yep! I'm glad you understand. And so does Mr Phillips, by the way. He's writing a script for a new play right now. It's about a vampire. And I'm going to play the main part. He says I look like a vampire.

MUM AND DAD (*laugh*)

DAD We'll be there! And you know what? I think we should go out now, and have dinner somewhere.

RUBY Sounds good, Dad. I'm really hungry. But I'm sorry – I'm not going to get changed.

MUM It doesn't matter. What matters is the kind of person you are, and not what you look like.

RUBY Thanks, Mum. (*they hug each other*)

DAD All right, and now let's go.

Teenage dramas

RUBY   Dad?
DAD   Yes?
RUBY   You do understand, don't you?
DAD   Yes I do!

20 The Bully

A teenage drama in 8 scenes

Roles	Min 10
Runtime	Around 7 minutes, depending on production
Sets	The school playground; Jacob's home; on the way to school; the classroom; the school office; the school computer room
Props	Rucksacks/schoolbags for kids and a pair of trainers for Jacob; several printouts of essays that the kids did as homework (on their computers); face paint to show a bruise on Jacob's face; if possible, an old keyboard that can be destroyed
Style	Modern drama
Synopsis	Harry's a bully. His main victim is Jacob, a shy boy in his class. Harry frequently ridicules Jacob in front of their classmates, who seem to feel uneasy about the way Jacob is treated by Harry but don't do anything about it – and occasionally, if reluctantly, join in when Harry teases his victim. In fact, when on occasion one of the kids tries to confront Harry, they themselves get threatened by him. When Jacob comes home one day with a bruise on his cheek, his mum starts becoming suspicious and she talks to Jacob's teacher, Mr Robinson. Then, when Harry breaks a keyboard in the computer room and forces Jacob to say it was him who'd broken it, the other children claim it was them who had broken it. When Mr Robinson asks Harry, he says he's got nothing to do with it – but when the teacher says that the computer room has a webcam and he will check, Harry knows he has gone too far …
Language level	Intermediate – B1
Language areas	*Something – anything – nothing – everything: Is there anything you've noticed? I won't say anything. Is there something you want to tell me? Everything's fine. It's nothing serious.* Language chunks: *What a waste of time! Come on, you lot! We're only kidding. That's none of your business. Nice try. What's going on? Leave me alone. Nothing serious. …, don't you think? I'll keep an eye on it. That's rubbish. What about you?*
Stage tips	Your students will be in familiar territory here as the acting style required is what they will have seen on any TV soap. Encourage them to be 'real' as there can be a tendency with this type of gritty drama to 'overact' which in turn can belittle the subject matter. One exercise you might try, to engender the feeling of alienation felt by the person who is bullied, is to get each one of them individually to stand in the

Teenage dramas

middle of a circle of the others and ask the others to really despise that person in the middle. They may giggle to begin with but ask them to try and get over that feeling and concentrate on what is the unpleasant task of summoning up negative feelings and concentrating them on one vulnerable individual trapped within the circle. Ask them to be as silent as possible to begin with and be really patient as eventually they will quieten and there will be an eerie and unpleasant atmosphere established. Let that linger until it becomes almost unbearable and then quietly allow them to hiss insults (within reason!) at the victim. One word such as 'idiot' repeated can be a powerful weapon. This will show how intense silence can be rather than histrionic overacting and although the hissed insults may sound barbaric it won't be long before someone giggles and it's ironically the best way to break the malevolent spell. The 'victim' shouldn't be allowed to say anything as the bullied are often voiceless although you may allow them to say and repeat the words 'Why?', 'Please' or 'Stop' when you feel the time is right. Once the spell is broken make sure the 'victim' is hugged by the others but ask them all to remember how it felt to bully and be bullied and add it to their emotional memory bank.

NB You might want to use this exercise at your own discretion, as certain students might feel uneasy about performing the activity.

Materials

Photocopiable Worksheet A p 213
- Comprehension
- Useful phrases

Photocopiable Worksheet B p 214
- Mini-dialogues
- *something/anything/ everything/nothing* etc.
- Creative writing: a letter asking for advice

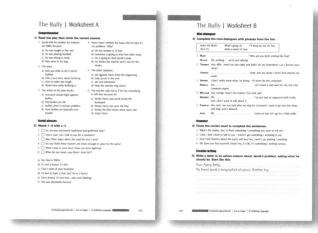

Teenage dramas

The Bully

Roles Harry, the bully Ruby
Jacob, the victim Lily
Oliver Katie
Jake Jacob's mum
Dylan Mr Robinson, teacher

Scene 1 **The school playground**

Seven kids with rucksacks are standing in a group, talking. Jacob enters, wearing new trainers. He wants to go past the group. School bell rings, a group of kids enter.

HARRY Another day over ... School – what a waste of time!

JAKE What shall we do?

KATIE Let's go to the park.

HARRY Ah, here's Jacob. Hi, Jacob. Why don't you join us?

DYLAN Hold on, Harry, I thought you didn't like Jacob.

HARRY I don't – just watch. Come on, Jacob!

JACOB OK.

HARRY Cool trainers. Really cool. No logo. I like that. Where did you buy them?

JACOB I didn't – my mum did.

HARRY Ah, your mum. (*to the others*) His mum did. She sure is an expert on trainers. (*singing*) Mummy bought cool trainers!

JACOB I like them.

HARRY He likes them. (*to the others*). Mummy bought cool trainers! Mummy bought cool trainers! Come on, you lot, join in.

KIDS (*rather reluctantly*) Mummy bought cool trainers! Mummy bought cool trainers!

JACOB Stop it!

HARRY Yeah, come on everyone. Stop it! We don't want to make Mummy's boy cry.

JACOB I'm not a Mummy's boy.

HARRY The problem is that your trainers look too new. But I can help you. (*grinding his foot on Jacob's trainers*) They look better now, don't they? Come on, you lot. Let Jacob go to Mummy.

The kids, led by Harry, start to leave.

DYLAN Don't worry, Jacob. We're only kidding.

Scene 2 **Jacob's home**

JACOB Hi, Mum.

Teenage dramas

JACOB'S MUM	Hi, Jacob. How was school?
JACOB	All right.
JACOB'S MUM	What did you do to your new trainers? They look filthy.
JACOB	I was playing football.
JACOB'S MUM	With your friends from school?
JACOB	Yes, with my friends from school. That's how they got dirty.

Scene 3   On the way to school

LILY	Have you done your essay, Harry?
HARRY	Not yet.
LILY	What do you mean 'Not yet'? We have to hand it in today.
HARRY	No problem.

Enter Jacob.

HARRY	Jacob, come here.
JACOB	What is it?
HARRY	Did you write the homework essay on your PC?
JACOB	Yeah, I always do. Why do you ask?
HARRY	Give me your essay.
JACOB	No, I can't do that.
HARRY	Just give it to me, or your new trainers will disappear.
JACOB	Here you are. (*hands over his essay and runs away*)
HARRY	(*walking back to Lily*) What did I tell you? Here's my homework.
LILY	But what about Jacob?
HARRY	That's none of your business.

Scene 4   The classroom

MR ROBINSON	Please put your essays on my desk.

Kids walk to the desk and put their essays on it.

MR ROBINSON	Jacob, what about your essay?
JACOB	Sorry sir, I … I …
MR ROBINSON	Well?
HARRY	He says he left it on the bus.
MR ROBINSON	Is that true, Jacob?
JACOB	Yes, sir, I left it on the bus.
MR ROBINSON	Nice try. Luckily you'll have plenty of time to write another one in detention.

Teenage dramas

LILY   (*quietly, to Harry*) That was mean.

HARRY   (*laughing*) Do you think so, Lily? OK. Maybe next time I'll take yours.

Scene 5   **The school playground**

Jacob is handing something over to Harry, but we can't see what it is. Oliver and Ruby are in the background.

HARRY   OK, remember – not a word to anyone!

JACOB   (*hesitantly*) No …

HARRY   (*grabbing Jacob*) You don't want me to get angry, right?

JACOB   I won't say anything. Promise!

Oliver and Ruby approach them.

OLIVER   What's going on?

HARRY   Nothing. (*releasing Jacob*) I was just having a chat with my friend Jacob. Isn't that right, Jacob?

JACOB   Yes, that's right.

OLIVER   Come on Harry, we're late for football. (*Exit Oliver and Harry*)

RUBY   What was that all about, Jacob?

JACOB   Nothing.

RUBY   Come on, Jacob. Tell me.

JACOB   He just wanted to borrow something.

RUBY   Borrow something?

JACOB   Yes, borrow something. (*Jacob runs off*)

Scene 6   **Jacob's home, some time later**

Enter Jacob.

JACOB'S MOTHER   Hi, Jacob!

JACOB   Hi, Mum.

JACOB'S MOTHER   What's happened to your face? There's a bruise on your cheek.

JACOB   I ran into a door.

JACOB'S MOTHER   Jacob, tell me – are there any problems at school?

JACOB   No, Mum, everything's fine.

JACOB'S MOTHER   Please tell me, Jacob, I know something's wrong.

JACOB   Leave me alone, Mum. I'm fine.

Scene 7   **The school office**

JACOB'S MOTHER   Thank you for seeing me, Mr Robinson.

Teenage dramas

MR ROBINSON   Not at all. Please sit down, Mrs Benson. What can I do for you?

JACOB'S MOTHER   I'm just a bit worried about Jacob's behaviour recently. Is there anything you've noticed?

MR ROBINSON   No, nothing serious. Just the usual jokes. And a boy should be able to take a joke, don't you think?

JACOB'S MOTHER   I agree, but yesterday there was a bruise on his cheek.

MR ROBINSON   Ah, what did he say about it?

JACOB'S MOTHER   He said he'd run into a door.

MR ROBINSON   But you don't believe him, right?

JACOB'S MOTHER   No, I don't.

MR ROBINSON   I understand what you're saying. I'll keep an eye on it.

JACOB'S MOTHER   Thank you, Mr Robinson.

MR ROBINSON   Goodbye, Mrs Benson.

Scene 8   The school computer room

All the kids are in the room; the teacher has left to get something.

HARRY   That keyboard's rubbish. Don't you think so, Jacob?

Harry starts breaking it.

DYLAN   Don't break it!

KATIE   Stop it, Harry! Mr Robinson will be furious with you.

Harry continues breaking the keyboard; the kids look on incredulously.

HARRY   Jacob, why did you break your keyboard?

JACOB   I didn't – you did!

RUBY   Harry, don't be silly. *You* did it!

HARRY   No, I didn't. Jacob did. And if any of you have a problem with that, you'd better say so now. Ruby? Dylan? Katie? Jake? Oliver?

Silence.

HARRY   No? Good.

Enter Mr Robinson.

MR ROBINSON   What was that noise?

The kids stay silent. Mr Robinson, looking around, spots the broken keyboard.

MR ROBINSON   Who broke the keyboard?

Kids stay silent.

MR ROBINSON   Jacob answer me. Who broke this keyboard?

Teenage dramas

Jacob	I did.
Mr Robinson	Jacob? You broke it?
Katie	That's not true, sir.
Mr Robinson	OK Katie, who *did* break it, then?
Katie	*I* did.
Dylan	No, *I* did.
Oliver	No, *I* did.
Jake	No, *I* did.
Ruby	No, *I* did.
Lily	No, *I* did.
Mr Robinson	OK, all of you. Wait for me at the headmaster's office.
Lily	Come on, Jacob.

She takes his arm and leads him out of the computer room; all the others except Harry follow her.

Mr Robinson	What about you, Harry?
Harry	Nothing to do with me, sir.
Mr Robinson	I hope not. Anyway we'll soon find out the truth.
Harry	What do you mean, sir?
Mr Robinson	Well, this computer's got a webcam. I switched it on before the lesson. Let's see what it recorded.
Harry	Sir?
Mr Robinson	What is it, Harry? Is there something you want to tell me?

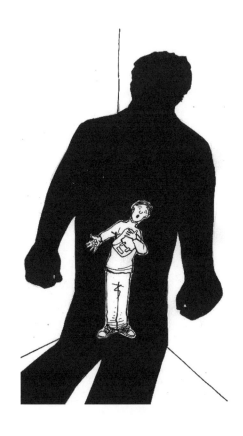

Teenage dramas

21 Friendship

Track 11–16

A teenage drama in 8 scenes

Roles	5–10 main characters (if you decide to double the roles); for the party (Scene 2) several more characters (non-speaking)
Runtime	Around 14 minutes, depending on production
Sets	Sheri's bedroom; a party; the school playground; the park; an art class; an art gallery
Props	Music for various scenes (to be chosen by the students); a football; sketchpads and pencils for the art class
Style	Modern teenage drama
Synopsis	Lisa and Sheri are best friends. When Sheri starts hanging out with Jamie and his friends, Lisa gets a little worried. She thinks that the 'football lads', as she calls them, are not the right company for her friend. But Sheri doesn't mind, as she finds Jamie so good-looking, and it doesn't take long for her to try to take Jamie away from Jenny, his girlfriend. Lisa warns her again, but Sheri doesn't want to listen. When Jenny hears what's going on, she is furious and tells Sheri off. Then, when Sheri crashes a party of the sixth-formers, things get really interesting – Jenny confronts Jamie, who claims he's not really interested in Sheri, and Sheri gets furious and starts screaming. The situation ends in an embarrassing way for Sheri …
Language level	Intermediate – B1
Language areas	Expressions to talk about people and relationships: *He's not really my type; He hangs out with the wrong crowd; You don't really fancy him, do you?; He's very interesting to talk to; They're the right/wrong crowd for you; he's good-looking; crash a party; keep away from someone; to have your say; to leave someone alone; to be grounded; to keep something a secret; to cheat on someone; she can be pretty tough; I was wondering whether you'd like some company; have a date with someone; to put up a fight; to be an item; to laugh something off; it's nothing serious; to make a fool of oneself; to lose a friend.*
Stage tips	The play begins with music playing. The choice of track should be made by the students in consultation with the teacher, but it's important that the lyrics should reflect the play's theme or mood – friendship, betrayal, truth – whatever the students decide once they've had a look at the play and checked out their favourite songs.

To mark the end of one scene and the beginning of another, extracts of the same songs or other ones should be chosen: 'Another Girl's Paradise' by Tori Amos |

Teenage dramas

would be a good choice for Scene 1, and for Scene 2 the choice could be 'Get The Party Started' by Pink.

At the end of Scene 2 it would be good to have music again, and something like 'Bad Girl' by Beyoncé would be very suitable – though it's important that the final choice is made by the students. If they would prefer they could sing the song choices themselves, unaccompanied.

Materials

 The concept of a "split scene"

Track 11–16

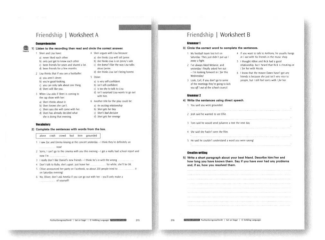

Photocopiable Worksheet A p 215

- Comprehension
- Vocabulary: relationships

Photocopiable Worksheet B p 216

- Phrasal verbs
- Direct/Indirect speech
- Creative writing: best friend

Teenage dramas

Friendship

Roles Sheri
Lisa, Sheri's friend
Dylan
Jamie
Jenny, Jamie's girlfriend
Jamie's friends
Announcer
Sheri's mother

Prelude *Play the music for a short time to set the scene, then enter Lisa from one side and Sheri from the other. The music gets quieter so that we can hear the dialogue, but continues as a background to the opening speeches. The actors address the audience.*

LISA Sheri has been my best friend for years and years. I think even as babies we were friends, when our mums took us to the park.

SHERI Lisa has been my best friend for ever. I'm a bit wild (or so my mum says) and I'm not always an easy person, I know that, but Lisa has always been my best friend.

LISA We cried together, we laughed together. I thought nothing would ever change.

SHERI But then, (*music stops*) there were some problems.

ANNOUNCER Scene 1: Sheri's bedroom.

Lisa and Sheri are sitting together, reading magazines, on the Internet, lying around, being teenagers! – then ...

LISA So what do you think of Alan?

SHERI He's cute but he's not really my type. And he hangs out with the wrong crowd.

LISA Like who?

SHERI Well, people who just aren't cool enough. You know, the ones who never get invited to parties. Like his friend Dylan – you know him, don't you?

Enter Dylan, who stands to one side looking out to audience. He's wearing glasses. Note: Dylan isn't with the girls; this is just a theatrical device to introduce this character to the audience.

LISA Yeah. He's in my art class. And I quite like him.

Dylan looks a little surprised but smiles to himself, takes his glasses off, and runs his fingers through his hair.

SHERI Oh come on, Lisa. You don't really fancy Dylan, do you?

Dylan's smile fades a little.

LISA I didn't say that, did I? But he's very interesting to talk to.

174 | PHOTOCOPIABLE | Puchta/Gerngross/Devitt | Get on Stage! | © Helbling Languages

Teenage dramas

Dylan now looks glummer – he wants to be 'fancied', not 'interesting to talk to'. He puts his glasses back on and exits.

SHERI OK, if you say so. Anyway, they're the wrong crowd for me.

LISA And what's the right crowd for you, then?

SHERI Jamie and his friends.

Jamie and a couple of friends enter on the opposite side from where Dylan left. They're carrying a football. They have 'attitude' – they strike a pose and jostle for position. Jamie wins. Again, they're not with the girls; it's as though they are in a thought bubble.

LISA What? The football lads? You can't be serious. They keep their brains in their boots!

Lads look rather pleased at this idea and nod in agreement.

SHERI I don't care – they've got nice legs, and Jamie's very good-looking, don't you think?

Jamie gives an 'of course I am!' look to the audience.

LISA But Sheri – all the guys can talk about is football.

Lads all shout 'offside' or 'goal' or any other football word the students might use to make the point.

SHERI (*laughs*) I don't care!

LISA Yeah, I can imagine. (*All the lads except Jamie exit as Jenny enters, she stands next to Jamie and takes his arm.*) Anyway, you know that he and Jenny are an item, don't you? (*Jamie and Jenny exit together.*)

SHERI And you don't think I can take him away from Jenny, do you? (*Now Sheri focuses on Jamie and Jenny as they exit.*)

LISA I didn't say that, did I? But she's two years older than you. I mean, why should Jamie be interested in a fifteen-year-old?

SHERI We'll see, Lisa ... we'll see.

LISA Sheri, you're not going to do anything stupid, are you?

SHERI Do I ever? (*they both laugh*)

Short snatch of music. Again, once the dialogue starts the music drops in volume but continues as a background to the scene. Jamie, his mates and anyone else (except Dylan) enter and form a group centre stage and dance – but they keep side-on or with their backs to the audience. Sheri joins them but faces the audience. Lisa stays to one side of the stage; she's not at the party but in the play she can still talk to Sheri. We are playing two 'realities' here, as in a film where there is a flashback and a voice-over continues in the present.

Sheri dances, but is looking for someone at the party. As she weaves in and out,

Teenage dramas

searching, the other characters can cast 'What's she doing here?' looks at her. If there are only a few other characters onstage, Sheri can peer into the audience as well, pretending they're part of the party crowd.

ANNOUNCER	(*who is now a partygoer*) Scene 2. A party!
LISA	(*from 'outside' the party*) What? You just went there?
SHERI	(*still looking*) Yeah! Why not?
LISA	You crashed the party? I've never heard of anybody our age crashing a sixth-form party.
SHERI	Well, I'm not just anybody, am I?
LISA	Still … Why didn't they kick you out?

Sheri sees Jamie and dances towards him. He has his back to the audience and doesn't see her coming.

SHERI	Jamie took care of me.
LISA	Jamie?
SHERI	Yeah, Jamie. I kind of bumped into him … (*she deliberately bumps into him, miming spilling coke on herself*)
JAMIE	Oh no! Sorry, sorry … I didn't see you. (*to Lisa*) And he spilled coke on my skirt. (*to Jamie*) Don't worry, Jamie. It was my fault.
JAMIE	I didn't know you knew any sixth–formers. What are you doing here?
SHERI	You don't mind me being here, do you?
JAMIE	(*smiling*) No, I don't mind.
SHERI	(*smiling as well*) Well, that's okay then isn't it?
JAMIE	I guess it is.
SHERI	(*to Lisa*) So we got talking a bit …
LISA	Where was Jenny all this time?
SHERI	(*to Lisa*) Jenny couldn't go to the party. (*to Jamie*) Where's Jenny tonight?
JAMIE	She's away on a course. Part of her studies, I think.
SHERI	Away? Really? I didn't know. (*but she obviously does*) So you're here all on your own?
JAMIE	(*considering*) Well, yes … I suppose I am.
SHERI	(*to Lisa*) So then we danced a bit … (*she and Jamie dance, then Sheri leaves Jamie and returns to Lisa*) … and then we kissed a bit …
LISA	Sheri! Are you crazy or something? What if Jenny finds out?
SHERI	Why should she? Jamie doesn't have to tell her, (*to Jamie*) do you?
JAMIE	I guess not.
LISA	But the others saw you, didn't they?

Teenage dramas

SHERI   Well just the dancing, not the kissing. So I think we're OK. Come on, Lisa, don't spoil it. (*Sheri and Jamie start to dance again.*) I'm having loads of fun!

Music as everyone exits except Lisa and Sheri, who dance to the front.

ANNOUNCER   Scene 3, in the school playground, a couple of days later.

Jenny enters. Music fades.

LISA   Look out! Jenny's coming and I don't think she's here to wish you happy birthday.

JENNY   (*to Sheri*) I'm only going to say this once. Keep away from Jamie!

SHERI   What are you talking about?

JENNY   Well, normally I wouldn't talk to a little nobody like you, but people said I should. So I hope you get the idea. Just keep away from him!

SHERI   Doesn't he have a say, too?

JENNY   Which part of 'keep away from him' don't you understand? I'm warning you! Leave him alone! (*she storms off*)

SHERI   (*aside*) We'll see!

LISA   Sheri – you heard her. You've got to forget about Jamie!

SHERI   Oh have I?

LISA   Yes! (*pause*) Look, are you coming to the rap show with me on Saturday?

SHERI   No, I can't. I'm grounded.

LISA   I could phone your mum and beg her to let you go. Tell her I've already got the tickets …

SHERI   It's not worth it. What makes you think she'd listen to you, anyway?

LISA   Hey, Sheri, what's the matter? I'm just trying to help!

SHERI   You don't have to rescue me all the time. (*there is a 'moment'*) All right – sorry I said that.

LISA   That's OK.

SHERI   Look. I've got to go now. See you around.

LISA   (*calling to Sheri as she leaves*) Think about Saturday, OK?

SHERI   I'll ring you.

Short snatch of music.

ANNOUNCER   (*entering and handing Lisa a mobile*) Scene 4, Saturday.

Lisa moves to the side of the stage and dials a number on her phone. We hear the sound of a phone ringing. On the opposite side of the stage to Lisa, Sheri's mother enters, with a phone. She answers.

LISA   Hi Mrs Paulton, it's Lisa.

SHERI'S MOTHER   Hi Lisa, how are things?

Puchta/Gerngross/Devitt | Get on Stage! | © Helbling Languages PHOTOCOPIABLE

Teenage dramas

LISA Fine, thanks. Can I talk to Sheri, please?

SHERI'S MOTHER I'm sorry, Lisa, she's not in. She went to a party. I'm surprised you didn't go together. Is everything all right?

LISA Yes, sure. I've got a ticket to a concert. Do you remember which party?

SHERI'S MOTHER Yeah, Carol. Carol Fielding. You know her, don't you?

LISA Sure. Thanks a lot. Bye.

SHERI'S MOTHER Bye. Have a good time.

(CD Track 14) *Music. Announcer enters and Lisa asks him/her a question. (The audience can't hear the question through the music, but it's 'Have you seen Sheri?') and the Announcer points to where Sheri has entered and is sitting down. The music fades as Lisa approaches Sheri.*

ANNOUNCER Scene 5. The park. Sunday.

LISA How's Carol?

SHERI What are you talking about?

LISA You lied to me. You said you were grounded.

SHERI How do you know?

LISA I phoned your place. I tried your mobile first but it was switched off.

SHERI All right. So I lied to you. I'm sorry.

LISA But why Carol? I mean, you don't even like her. And she doesn't like you. Why go to her party?

SHERI I didn't.

LISA But your mum ...

SHERI I told my mum I was at Carol's party. But I wasn't.

LISA So where were you?

SHERI I was with Jamie. At his house.

LISA What! I don't believe it. Didn't Jenny tell you to keep away?

SHERI *(mocking)* 'Didn't Jenny tell you to keep away'? Anyway, she's out of town.

LISA But what's she going to say when she gets back?

SHERI Say about what? We aren't going to tell her, are we? Jamie said we should keep it a secret from Jenny.

LISA And you agreed?

SHERI Why shouldn't I? He's so cool.

LISA But it's wrong!

SHERI Dammit, Lisa – stop telling me what to do!

LISA No, it's wrong of Jamie, too. Don't you see? He's cheating on Jenny – and he's cheating on you, too, isn't he?

SHERI	That's fine with me. I don't mind. As long as I can see him.
LISA	But Sheri – Jamie's cheating!
SHERI	Stop talking about him like that.
LISA	Sheri, please.
SHERI	If you're my friend, Lisa, you'll let me be with Jamie and stop talking about it.
LISA	And if I don't?
SHERI	Well, Jamie is more important to me right now.
LISA	Are you saying … ?
SHERI	Yes, I am. Think about it. Bye.

Music. Announcer enters and hands Lisa a sketchpad and pencil. Dylan enters with sketchpad and pencil. Lisa and Dylan sit and start to sketch. Announcer strikes a pose at one side of the stage, downstage. He/she is the model they are sketching in their life-drawing class. Music fades.

ANNOUNCER	Scene 6. The art class. Some weeks later.
DYLAN	How come I never see you with Sheri any more?
LISA	Well, she's got different things to do. I haven't spoken to her for weeks.
DYLAN	Pity. She seemed kind of fun.
LISA	Yeah, she is. I mean, she was.
DYLAN	She's hanging out with the football crowd now, isn't she?
LISA	Hmmm, yes, looks like it.
DYLAN	I've heard a rumour that she's after Jamie. She'd better be careful – Jenny isn't someone I'd want as an enemy.
LISA	Well, I hope she knows what she's doing. But Sheri can be pretty tough too.
DYLAN	If you say so. (*pause*) Um … Lisa? There's an exhibition of Da Vinci sketches and sculptures at the Royal Academy. Were you thinking of going?
LISA	Yes, I was. Why?
DYLAN	Well, I was wondering whether you'd like have to company.
LISA	Well, yes. I wonder who I could go with?
DYLAN	(*a little crestfallen*) Oh …
LISA	I'm joking, Dylan! I'd love it if you came with me.
DYLAN	Really?
LISA	Really really!
DYLAN	Wow! Don't worry – it's not a proper date or anything. You don't have to tell anyone we're going together or anything if you're embarrassed or anything.
LISA	(*laughing*) Don't worry. I'll wear a disguise!

Teenage dramas

DYLAN (*gathering up his things, but making a mess of it in his excitement. He laughs but then has a thought*) You are joking about the disguise, aren't you?

LISA Of course!

DYLAN Brilliant! See you Saturday, then!

LISA (*getting up too*) I'm looking forward to it already.

DYLAN Really?

LISA Yes! Yes! Yes! Really! See you Saturday.

Music. They exit. Announcer enters in a black cap or similar, to denote he/she is a gallery attendant.

ANNOUNCER Shhhh! (*music stops abruptly*) Don't you know this is an art gallery? Scene 7. The Royal Academy. Saturday.

Dylan and Lisa enter with the exhibition leaflet. As the dialogue progresses they move across the stage, pretending to go from one artwork to another on the wall referring to the leaflet. Sheri, Jamie and Jenny also enter, and pose like a Da Vinci sculpture with Jenny pointing angrily at Sheri who stands defiantly. Jamie stands between them trying to placate them. Jenny and Sheri 'come alive' for their lines, but when Dylan and Lisa are speaking they freeze again. Dylan and Lisa remain oblivious to the drama; they keep on looking at the paintings.

DYLAN You mean Sheri didn't phone you?

LISA No, she didn't. Why? What happened?

DYLAN Well, it seems Sheri crashed Jenny's party, and when Jenny saw her she shouted:

JENNY What's she doing here? Get her out!

DYLAN But Sheri put up a fight and she shouted for Jamie. When Jamie came over to her, she told everybody ...

SHERI Jamie only loves me. He and Jenny aren't an item any more.

LISA Oh my God! What did Jamie say?

DYLAN What do you think? Nothing at all! But Jenny was furious. She wanted Jamie to ...

JENNY Tell me whether you love me or not.

DYLAN In front of all the others. Or ...

JENNY Is it true what Sheri's saying?

LISA And?

DYLAN Well, he tried to laugh it off, but Jenny wouldn't let him.

LISA And?

DYLAN So Jamie said ...

JAMIE	I only want you, Jenny. Yes, I met Sheri once or twice, but it was nothing serious.
DYLAN	Then Sheri started screaming …
SHERI	You're a liar!
DYLAN	– and some other things, too. (*Announcer and one of Jamie's mates grab Sheri and march her off. Jamie and Jenny follow them.*) Then two of Jamie's friends picked Sheri up and threw her out. But she went on screaming and started throwing stones at the windows. So some neighbours phoned the police, and they picked her up and drove her home and gave her a warning, I think.
LISA	Oh, no. Poor Sheri!
DYLAN	Poor Sheri? It was all her fault, wasn't it?
LISA	Well, all she did was fall in love. That's not a crime, is it? I feel a bit sorry for her, I must say.
DYLAN	Yeah, I guess you're right. I'll see you in the next room.

Track 12

He exits as Sheri enters. Lisa and Sheri return to the positions they were at the beginning of the play, facing the audience.

Music, probably same as the opening music, as a background to the last two speeches.

LISA	(*to audience*) As I said, I thought nothing would ever change. But things have changed. Does that mean you can lose a friend so easily? Just because of a boy – a boy like Jamie! Maybe I should phone her …
SHERI	I've made a real fool of myself. And I need someone to talk to about it. But I've lost my best friend, too. Maybe I'll phone her. Maybe she'll listen to me …

They look at each other across the stage. Music swells. Curtain.

Photocopiable Worksheets

The Perfect Son | Worksheet

Comprehension

1) Listen to the recording then match 1–6 with a–f.

1 ☐ The boy never forgets to do it.   a) the truth
2 ☐ These are never bad.   b) great
3 ☐ He never uses this.   c) early
4 ☐ He always tells this.   d) his homework
5 ☐ This is when he always comes home.   e) his marks
6 ☐ The man thinks his son is this.   f) bad language

Vocabulary

2) We hear the words 'perfect', 'great' and 'fantastic' in the sketch. Tick six words in the list below that have a similar meaning.

☐ useless   ☐ outstanding   ☐ impossible
☐ enthusiastic   ☐ superb   ☐ brilliant
☐ excellent   ☐ intelligent   ☐ attractive
☐ boring   ☐ expensive   ☐ wonderful
☐ practical   ☐ awesome   ☐ interesting
☐ legal   ☐ comfortable

Grammar

3) Circle the correct form of the verb.

1 Does your friend never *gets / get* bad marks at school?
2 Kitty sometimes *forgets / forget* to do her homework.
3 My sister never *tells / tell* a lie!
4 Joshua doesn't *uses / use* bad language.
5 Steve *come / comes* home late every Friday.

4) Complete the sentences with the correct form of the verb in brackets.

1 Our maths teacher never .... (give) us homework.
2 .... your father ever .... (get) angry?
3 Matt always .... (play) football on Saturday.
4 Mum often .... (take) me shopping at the weekend.
5 Sally sometimes .... (watch) TV in the evening.

Smart Shoppers | Worksheet

Comprehension

1) **Listen to the recording then read and circle (T) True or (F) False.**

   1 The woman is trying on a new dress.   T / F
   2 The man is bored.   T / F
   3 He thinks the woman looks good.   T / F
   4 They look at shoes in the shop.   T / F
   5 The shopkeeper likes the green scarf.   T / F
   6 The woman tries a skirt on.   T / F
   7 They pay for the coat.   T / F

Dialogue

2) **Complete the dialogue with the phrases from the box.**

take them   try them   to match   gorgeous   Let's go   doesn't go

Jack	I've got a new shirt – what do you think?
Ellie	Wow, that's great! But it ¹................................ with your trousers.
Jack	Oh! So I need some new trousers, too.
Ellie	And I want a coat! ²................................ shopping!
Ellie	These look nice.
Assistant	Hello, can I help you?
Ellie	Yes. I love those ³................................ scarves. Can I see one?
Assistant	Yes, here you are.
Jack	Oh, I really like these trousers!
Ellie	Yes, they look fantastic, but ⁴................................ first.
Jack	No. I'm sure they're OK. I'll ⁵................................ .
Assistant	Thank you, sir.
Jack	Now I want some shoes ⁶................................ .

Useful phrases

3) **Circle the correct phrase to complete the sentences.**

   1 *Calm down / You're calm*! Don't be so angry!
   2 I'm so bored! I know, *let's go / we go* to the cinema this evening.
   3 Hmm, I don't like this green dress. Could you *hand me / hand* the blue one, please?
   4 *Hurry up / Don't hurry*, we're late!
   5 *What's the matter? / Do you matter?* Is there something wrong?

A Fast-Food Stall | Worksheet

Comprehension

1) **Listen to the recording then read and circle (T) True or (F) False.**

   1 All the customers are polite at the beginning.   T / F
   2 The first customer is not interested in the colour of the plate. T / F
   3 The assistant wants to serve the first customer quickly.   T / F
   4 The assistant acts differently with the second customer.   T / F
   5 The assistant is quick with the orders.   T / F
   6 Customers 4, 5 and 6 are pleased with the service.   T / F

Mini- dialogues

2) **Complete the mini-dialogues with phrases from the box.**

   | It doesn't matter | let's come | was quick |
   | Please hurry | Here we are | Great service |

   1 **A** The cinema is dark, I can't see my friends – where are you all?
      B .... ! Now hurry up and sit down, the film's going to start!

   2 **Waiter** Here you are madam, your drinks.
      Naomi   Wow, that .... ! We only ordered a minute ago!

   3 **Waiter** Would you like ketchup or mustard with your burger?
      Jeff   .... , I like both!

   4 **Poppy**   .... , I have to leave soon.
      Waiter Sorry madam, we have a problem in the kitchen!

   5 **Waiter** Here's your meal, sir.
      Mike   Oh, that's fantastic! .... ! I love this place.

   6 **Sally**   Oh, this is lovely. I'm really enjoying my meal.
      Paul   Me too. I know, ... here for your birthday!
      Sally   Great idea!

Useful phrases

3) **Match 1–6 with a–f.**

   1 ☐ It's too hot in here!   a) We should come here again.
   2 ☐ The view is fabulous.   b) What about asking Jane for help?
   3 ☐ I want to talk to Josh about the match.   c) How about a pizza?
   4 ☐ What shall we have for lunch?   d) Let's go and sit outside.
   5 ☐ I don't know how to do this homework.   e) Well, he could go to Italy.
   6 ☐ Jack doesn't know where to go on holiday.   f) Why don't you call him now?

Colin the Poet | Worksheet

Comprehension

1) **Listen to the recording then read and circle (T) True or (F) False.**

   1 Colin's family are tired of his rhyming. T / F
   2 Colin wants coffee, toast and cheese for his breakfast. T / F
   3 Fred wants brown toast. T / F
   4 Kate has some orange juice. T / F
   5 Colin wins a trip to America. T / F
   6 Another title for the play could be *We all like Colin now*! T / F

Vocabulary

2) **Reorder the letters to make words about breakfast. Then write them under the correct picture.**

   1 satto
   2 drife geg
   3 hesece
   4 drabe
   5 nagore ujeci
   6 redalamma
   7 mja
   8 eutrbt

1 .... 2 .... 3 .... 4 ....

5 .... 6 .... 7 .... 8 ....

Dialogue

3) **Complete the dialogue with words or phrases from the box.**

| just   Do you   Would you like   some   yes, please |

DAD Hi Andrew, finally! You're late!
ANDREW Sorry everyone! What's for breakfast?
DAD ¹.................................. some toast?
ANDREW Oh, ²........................... .
DAD One slice or two?
ANDREW Two, please, I'm hungry!
DAD Here's your toast. ³.................................. want some tea?

ANDREW No thanks. I want ⁴.................................. orange juice, please. Or perhaps milk … no, orange juice.
DAD Marlene, how about you?
MARLENE Oh, ⁵.................................. some tea, please.
DAD Anything to eat?
MARLENE No thanks.

The Ticket | Worksheet

Comprehension

1) Listen to the recording then read and circle the correct answer.

1 The woman seems:
  a) angry.
  b) impatient.
  c) nice.
  d) bored.

2 The man:
  a) didn't stop at the lights.
  b) was driving too fast.
  c) stopped too quickly.
  d) wasn't driving.

3 The woman:
  a) is angry with the officer.
  b) is irritated with her husband.
  c) is upset.
  d) thinks her husband is funny.

4 The man:
  a) is angry with his wife.
  b) apologises to the officer.
  c) laughs with the officer.
  d) insults the officer.

5 The woman:
  a) is angry with the officer.
  b) laughs at the policemen.
  c) shouts at her husband.
  d) agrees with the officer.

6 At the end:
  a) the officer is cleverer than the man.
  b) the man is cleverer.
  c) the woman goes to prison.
  d) the man was right.

Mini-dialogues

2) Complete the mini-dialogues with words from the box.

| warning   jumping   losing   giving   insulting   saying |

1 **Man** What's the problem, officer? I haven't done anything wrong!
  Officer I'm .... you a ticket for driving too fast.

2 **Jenny** Look, I'm sorry for .... your phone! I'll buy you another one.
  Fred No, that's OK, it was only an old one.

3 **Man** Officer, I haven't got time to talk to you, I'm in a hurry!
  Officer I'm .... you sir, you must speak to me politely.

4 **Jerry** I told the police officer she was stupid.
  Mike You idiot! Why did you do that? What happened then?
  Jerry She arrested me for .... a police officer.

5 **Tom** I don't know what Bill said, but Sophie's really angry!
  Lynn Oh, no. Bill makes everyone angry and just says 'I'm only .... what I think'!

6 **Lisa** What's wrong with Jane? She doesn't look very happy!
  Cath Yes, she was driving her dad's car this morning – he was really angry with her for .... a red light.

Being Polite | Worksheet

Comprehension

1) Watch the video of the play then read and circle the correct answer.

1 When the shopkeeper says 'sorry', to the first customer, he or she:
   a) is apologising.
   b) is asking the customer to repeat what he said in a different way.
   c) is telling the customer to be quiet.
   d) hasn't heard the customer.

2 The customer:
   a) doesn't think he needs to be polite.
   b) thinks the shopkeeper is being rude.
   c) thinks he needs a magic word.
   d) thinks he's said the magic word.

3 When the first customer finally asks politely, he:
   a) is still angry.
   b) still doesn't know what the shopkeeper is talking about.
   c) feels better than he did when he came into the shop.
   d) still doesn't want to be polite.

4 When the second customer arrives, the first customer:
   a) encourages him to be rude.
   b) is still in a hurry.
   c) is very helpful.
   c) leaves.

5 The third customer is very polite:
   a) so he is served immediately.
   b) but he has also come to the wrong shop.
   c) but not polite enough.
   d) so in the end everyone is satisfied.

6 A good title for the play would be:
   a) How to buy a saw
   b) Buying shoes
   c) The deaf shopkeeper
   d) Learning a lesson

Useful phrases

2) Complete the table with one of the requests below.

1 very impolite	
2 impolite	
3 neutral	I'd like a large fish and some chips.
4 polite	
5 more polite	
6 very polite	

Could you possibly pass the butter, please?
Good morning. I'd like some cola, please.
Get me two packets of crisps, right now.
Would you mind getting me a bar of chocolate?
Get me a kilo of apples.
~~I'd like a large fish and some chips.~~

Parrot Learns a Lesson | Worksheet

Comprehension.

1) Listen to the recording then read and circle the correct answer.

1. John puts Percy in the cupboard because:
   a) that's where Percy lives.
   b) Percy likes it in there.
   c) Percy has been impolite.
   d) he doesn't want anyone to see Percy.

2. When Percy is rude, the first thing John does is:
   a) threaten him.
   b) put him somewhere unpleasant.
   c) laugh at him.
   d) hit him.

3. Percy is:
   a) rude to men, but polite to women.
   b) only rude to John.
   c) polite to everyone.
   d) rude to John's guests.

4. Before his boss arrives, John expects Percy:
   a) to behave well.
   b) to be funny.
   c) to say rude things.
   d) to stay silent.

5. When Percy comes out of the freezer, he wants to:
   a) use bad words.
   b) have dinner.
   c) know about the frozen chickens in the freezer.
   d) go to bed.

6. Percy thinks the chickens are in the freezer because:
   a) they've been impolite.
   b) John is going to eat them.
   c) they live there.
   d) John has forgotten about them.

Mini-dialogues

2) Complete these mini-dialogues with words from the box.

| course | to | way | into | lesson | right |

1. **Dave** Hello, Sam, did you have a nice journey?
   Sam Hi, Dave, good .... see you. The journey was great, thanks.

2. **Jill** Carol, did you remember to lock the door?
   Carol Of .... I did! You know I never forget things like that!

3. **Paul** Wow, Jim, what have you done to your head?
   Jim I fell off my bike, and I wasn't wearing a helmet. But I've learnt my .... – I'll always wear it now!

4. **Holly** Dad, can I watch the film on TV later this evening?
   Dad What? There's no .... I'm going to let you watch a film like that!

5. **Patricia** Hi, Gemma, it's me, Patty!
   Gemma Oh, hi Patty, come .... in!

6. **Jackie** Come on, forget about the homework. Let's go and hang out in the shopping centre.
   Tara No, you know we'll get .... trouble with Mr Simpson if we don't do it.

Granddad's Birthday | Worksheet

Comprehension

1) **Listen to the recording then read and circle the correct answer.**

1. Lily is giving Granddad a:
   a) parrot.   c) Rolls with a driver.
   b) poem.   d) painting.

2. At first, Mark:
   a) hasn't decided what to give granddad.
   b) had the idea of giving him a painting.
   c) wants to paint a picture for him.
   d) wants to give him a valuable object.

3. How does everyone feel about their presents?
   a) uncertain.   c) not interested.
   b) confident.   d) bored.

4. They want to make their granddad feel:
   a) surprised.   c) happy.
   b) angry.   d) amazed.

5. Granddad didn't like the car because:
   a) it was too old.
   b) he doesn't need one.
   c) the gardener's son needed one.
   d) he didn't like the colour.

6. Granddad liked the parrot:
   a) because he thought it was funny.
   b) because it was delicious to eat.
   c) because it talked to him.
   d) because he could sell it.

Mini-dialogues

2) **Complete the mini-dialogues with phrases from the box.**

| how did you like | so I took it | Why don't you |
| so I said | I'm going to | did she like |

1. **Manny**   Isn't it Julie's birthday soon?
   Heather   Yes, I need to buy a present today.
   Manny   ¹............................... give her some perfume?
   Heather   Hmm. Perfume's OK, I suppose …

   (A week later)
   Manny   So ²............................... her present?
   Heather   She loved it! I was so pleased!

2. **Sandra**   Well, ³............................... the restaurant Nat took you to?
   Michelle   It was horrible! I hope it wasn't your idea!

3. **Charlie**   What happened to that new shirt you bought?
   Pete   Oh, I decided I didn't like the colour, ⁴............................... back to the shop.

4. **Kate**   Hi, Samantha – I hear you went to the cinema with Ryan yesterday.
   Samantha   That's right! He asked me at school, and I really like him, ⁵............................... yes!

5. **Sandra**   Come on Angela, switch off the computer and let's go out!
   Angela   No, ⁶............................... play this game until I get to the next level!

The Princess and the Ring | Worksheet

Comprehension

1) **Listen to the recording then read and circle (T) True or (F) False.**

   1 Rita is very serious about being a princess. T / F
   2 Humphrey thinks Flora should dress more appropriately. T / F
   3 Rita won't help Flora because she can't swim. T / F
   4 Flora likes the otter prince. T / F
   5 The otter prince has a castle next to the football stadium. T / F
   6 Neither sister finds a suitable partner. T / F

Vocabulary

2) **Complete the sentences with the words from the box.**

   | drop   bushes   scruffy   hooligan   swamp   fault |

   1 Sarah spent ages looking for her golf ball in the .... next to the golf course.
   2 I don't want to go to the football match with Conor – when he's with his friends he becomes a real ....
   3 Those signs on the map mean that area is wet and muddy – it's a .... , in fact.
   4 Don't shout at John, I broke your computer, it's my ....
   5 My dog never looks clean and tidy, he's always so ....
   6 Be careful with that old cup – please don't .... it, it's very valuable.

Grammar

3) **Complete the sentences with words or phrases from the box.**

   | can't   are allowed   can't   aren't allowed   can   can |

   1 DANGER – DEEP WATER – NO SWIMMING
      You .... to swim here.
   2 *Private restaurant – no trainers – jackets and ties only*
      You .... go in there without a tie.
   3 Tourist maps of the city – please take one.
      You .... take a map if you want one.
   4 'It's no use – my arm isn't long enough to reach the ring at the bottom of the pond.'
      I .... get the ring, the pond is too deep.
   5 PETS PERMITTED IN THIS PARK
      You .... to take your dog into the park.
   6 ENGLISH AND FRENCH SPOKEN IN THIS SHOP!
      I speak English, so I .... talk to the assistant here.

At the Doctor's | Worksheet A

Comprehension

1) Read the play then circle the correct answer.

1. The doctor gives the first patient orange juice:
   a) to cure the problem.
   b) because the patient asks for some.
   c) so the doctor can see where the problem is.
   d) because vampires don't like it.

2. When the doctor sees the second patient, he is:
   a) understanding.
   b) unsympathetic.
   c) encouraging.
   d) angry.

3. When the woman talks about her husband:
   a) at first the doctor thinks there's nothing wrong.
   b) the doctor immediately knows what's wrong.
   c) the doctor gives her some medicine.
   d) the doctor thinks it's funny.

4. The nurse:
   a) suggests some medicine.
   b) tells the woman to bring her husband.
   c) asks the woman for some eggs.
   d) offers to build him a nice nest.

5. The old man is a little:
   a) deaf.
   b) blind.
   c) silly.
   d) tired.

6. The last patient:
   a) is bitten by Patient 1.
   b) bites the doctor.
   c) takes some coloured pills.
   d) does some ironing.

Useful phrases

2) Match 1–6 with a–f.

1. ☐ Oh dear, I don't think I'll go to school today.
2. ☐ I find it difficult to walk at the moment.
3. ☐ You'll have to say all that again.
4. ☐ I don't know why, but I can't sleep.
5. ☐ Look at these red spots on my leg!
6. ☐ I played tennis all day yesterday.

a) Now my arm hurts!
b) I'm afraid I can't hear very well.
c) Oh yes! I think you've been bitten!
d) It's because I have a swollen leg.
e) What's the matter? Don't you feel well?
f) What's wrong with me, doctor?

At the Doctor's | Worksheet B

Mini-dialogues

3) Complete the mini-dialogues with the letters of the phrases below.

a) do a test   c) patient   e) call an ambulance
b) take a pill d) make an appointment f) prescription

1 **Max**   Oh, I've got a terrible headache!
  Nurse   Here, ... , you'll feel better in a few minutes.
2 **Nurse**   Good morning, Doctor, there's a .... outside waiting to see you.
  Doctor   Thank you, Nurse, please send her in.
3 **Mr Perkins** Well, Doctor, what's my problem?
  Doctor   To be honest, I don't know. I think you'll have to ....
4 **Mrs Williams** So, Doctor, what do I have to do?
  Doctor   I want you to drink some of this medicine twice a day. I'll give you a .... and you can get some from the chemist's on your way home.
5 **Receptionist** (*on phone*) Hello, Mr Atkins. Is your problem serious?
  Mr Atkins No, I just want the doctor to sign a form for me.
  Receptionist OK, if you .... you can see him tomorrow evening.
6 **Man**   Oh, look, that man there has fallen over. I think he's broken his leg!
  Woman   Quick, somebody .... !

Grammar

4) Complete the sentences with the correct form of the verb in brackets.

1 I was ironing when the phone .... (ring)
2 Shelly .... to Denise when Tom asked if she wanted to dance. (talk)
3 Paul was buying a ticket when the train .... the station. (leave)
4 Shannon .... her e-mail when the screen went blank. (read)
5 Coral and Anna .... when Tim saw them in the cafe. (argue)
6 We .... outside when it started to rain. (stand)

Useful phrases

5) Match 1–6 with a–f.

1 ☐ What's all this glass on the floor?   a) She has hurt her leg.
2 ☐ Why is Gemma crying?   b) Patty has told them a really good joke.
3 ☐ Isn't your dog here?   c) Oh, Ian has burnt the steaks on the barbecue!
4 ☐ What's that smell?
5 ☐ Why are Pauline and Rhianna laughing?   d) Emma has said she'll go out with him!
                                                e) I've broken a window.
6 ☐ Why does Jack look so happy?   f) No, he's run away.

On Holiday in Rome | Worksheet A

Comprehension

1) **Listen to the recording then read and circle (T) True or (F) False.**

   1 There are lots of hotels like this one in England. T / F
   2 Mr and Mrs Davies last came here 20 years ago. T / F
   3 Mr and Mrs Davies ask if they can eat at the hotel. T / F
   4 They go and eat in a burger restaurant. T / F
   5 Mr and Mrs Davies would like a holiday abroad. T / F
   6 Mrs Davies didn't want to say she had won the lottery. T / F
   7 Ms Wilson thinks going to Rome is a good idea. T / F
   8 Mr and Mrs Davies leave Rome because they don't like eating late. T / F

Dialogue

2) **Complete the dialogue with phrases from the box.**

| that's unbelievable | a bite to eat | What's it about? |
| So was I | We certainly would | I'm afraid I can't tell you |

WOMAN Come on, it's time for lunch. This place looks nice, and there's a little jazz band playing inside. Let's get ¹.. .

MAN OK. We'll go inside. Excuse me, what's on the menu today?

WAITER ².. . The chef hasn't arrived yet so we don't know what he's going to cook! I'm afraid you'll have to wait a few minutes – I'm sure he'll be here soon!

WOMAN But, ³.. . Still, I suppose we can have something to drink until he comes.

WAITER Would you like to see what drinks we have?

MAN ⁴.. . It's hot outside and I'm very thirsty!

WOMAN Well, if we have to wait then I'm going to read my book for a while.

MAN It looks interesting. ⁵.. ?

WOMAN It's a restaurant guide for this city! I'm looking for somewhere to eat this evening!

(later)

WOMAN Oh, that was good! I was so hungry!

MAN ⁶.. ! But it's not surprising, we waited for an hour before the chef arrived!

On Holiday in Rome | Worksheet B

Dialogue

3) Complete the dialogue with the correct question tags from the box.

| haven't you | will she | could you | can't they | isn't she | don't you |

SARAH Oh dear, Jane lent me her new sweater yesterday and now there's some chocolate on the front. She's going to be really angry, ¹.............................?

AMANDA Yes, she is. You know what she's like!

SARAH Yes. I think I'll take the sweater to the cleaners – they can help me, ².............................?

AMANDA Probably. Anyway, it's only chocolate. You've got enough money for the bus, ³.............................?

SARAH Oh, I'd forgotten about that. You couldn't lend me a pound, ⁴.............................?

AMANDA Yes, here you are. You're lucky I haven't spent it yet!

SARAH Oh, I hope it'll be OK. If they can't do anything she'll never talk to me again, ⁵.............................?

AMANDA No. Oh, Sarah, you know Jane's standing just behind us, ⁶.............................?

Creative writing

4) A friend of yours has come for a visit. Write the conversation you have when you meet him/her, for example:

- *You haven't changed a bit, have you?*
- *Your parents are moving house, aren't they?*

You should also use the language you have seen in this unit. Here are a few ideas:

- *It's so good to see you again.*
- *It's so good to be back.*

At the Hairdresser's | Worksheet A

Comprehension

1) Read the play then match 1–6 with a–f.

1 ☐ At first the hairdresser thinks
2 ☐ The girl says she can
3 ☐ After his haircut the bald man
4 ☐ When he sees it, the second customer
5 ☐ When Knuckles comes into the shop
6 ☐ When the police officer returns, the hairdresser

a) he isn't looking for a haircut.
b) hates his new haircut.
c) thinks he has more hair than before.
d) help the hairdresser make more money.
e) tells him to come back another time.
f) the girl has come for a haircut.

Vocabulary

2) Complete the sentences with words from the box.

| bargain   hairdo   recognises   customer   robber   creative |

1 Someone who comes into a shop to buy something is a ....
2 A person who steals things is a ....
3 When you use new ideas in your work, you are being ....
4 The way you have your hair is called a ....
5 If something costs a lot less than you expected then it's a ....
6 The hairdresser knows who Knuckles is when he walks into the shop because he .... him.

Dialogue

3) Complete the dialogue with the correct letter of the phrases below.

a) Wait and see
b) get cutting
c) no funny business
d) ~~Are you crazy~~
e) might as well
f) an expert in

MARK Hi Sally. Do you want to come and watch the school football team?
SALLY ¹..d..? Look at the weather! I don't want to stand in the rain all morning!
MARK Well, if you don't want to do that then we ²......... stay at home and watch TV.
SALLY No, I've got a great idea!
MARK What are you looking for?
SALLY ³.........!
MARK What's this? Towel, scissors …
SALLY I'm going to give you a new hairdo! Is that OK?
MARK Well, yes. But ⁴......... . I want to look good when we go out tonight.
SALLY You didn't know I'm ⁵......... hairdressing, did you?
MARK No, I didn't. But stop talking and ⁶.........!

At the Hairdresser's | Worksheet B

Grammar 1

4) Complete the sentences in the conditional with the correct form of the verbs in brackets.

1 You would like Kitty's boyfriend if you .... him. (meet)
2 If she had woken up earlier she .... the bus. (catch)
3 If your dad .... you his car we'll go to the festival tomorrow. (lend)
4 If you cook dinner tonight I .... the washing up. (do)
5 If you .... me a text I would have known about the party! (send)
6 Danny .... you more if you smiled! (like)

Grammar 2

5) Rewrite the sentences using the correct form of the verb in brackets.

Example *I bought my bike two years ago.*
I've had my bike for two years. (have)

1 She arrived at the restaurant an hour ago.
  She .... an hour. (be)
2 He started work as a hairdresser ten years ago.
  He .... ten years. (be)
3 We've had our dog for a long time now.
  We .... (get)
4 Michael met Connie ages ago.
  Michael .... (know)

Creative writing

6) You see this advert in a music magazine. Write an e-mail to Julie, telling her why you think you'd be a good person for the job. Talk about:

- *where you've worked*
- *who you have worked with*
- *why you think you'd be a good person for the team*

WANTED
Hair stylist to the stars!
We need a young hair stylist to join our team. We send stylists out on tour with top music artists. We need energetic, creative and fun people to help us!

Send an e-mail now to Julie, at:
julie.edwards@starstyle.com

....
....
....
....
....

The Space Restaurant | Worksheet A

Comprehension

1) Watch the video of the play then read and circle the correct answer.

1 'Take a seat.' means:
   a) You take this chair home.
   b) Please sit down.

2 If the waiter says 'Can I take your coats?', he means:
   a) 'Can I hang your coat up for you?'
   b) 'You should hang your coats up.'

3 When you want to order a drink you say:
   a) 'I want cola.'
   b) 'I'll have a cola.'

4 Dorothy doesn't write down the drinks orders because:
   a) she doesn't understand the customers.
   b) the customers order too quickly for her.

5 Lamb is from:
   a) a sheep   b) a hen

6 There are no knives or forks in the restaurant because it is:
   a) for astronauts.
   b) in space.

Vocabulary

2) Match the definition with the correct word.

1 ☐ the meat from cows   a) sheep
2 ☐ the animal lamb comes from   b) smoothie
3 ☐ the meat from hens   c) soup
4 ☐ you eat this, but it's liquid   d) beef
5 ☐ a thick drink made of real fruit   e) chicken

Useful phrases

3) Match 1–6 with a–f.

1 ☐ Do you have a table for five people?
2 ☐ Can I see what kind of food you serve here?
3 ☐ Would you like something to drink?
4 ☐ Are you ready to order?
5 ☐ Can you pass me some bread, please?
6 ☐ Could you bring me a smoothie, please?

a) Thanks, I'll have a cola.
b) Yes sir, I'll be right back with it.
c) Of course, here you are.
d) Yes, madam. Here's a menu for you.
e) Yes, of course. Please take a seat here.
f) Yes, we are. We'll have the beef.

The Space Restaurant | Worksheet B

Grammar 1

4) Complete the sentences with the correct word from the box.

| ours   yours   mine   his   theirs   hers |

1 I bought that CD last week. It's ....
2 My dad gave my brother and me that TV for Christmas. It's ....
3 I'm sure this isn't my dictionary. Oh yes, here's Jenny's name on the front page. It's ....
4 I'm sure this is the scarf I gave you for your birthday. Yes, it's ....
5 I think that desk is where James and Nick sit. Yes, it's ....
6 My brother says the laptop is .... , but it belongs to both of us.

Grammar 2

5) Complete the sentences with the correct form of the verb in brackets.

1 'This is nice – I can .... (taste) lamb.'
2 'Who ordered beef?' 'We .... (do).'
3 'Are you ready to order?'
  'Yes. My children .... (have) an orange juice and a lemonade.'
4 'Have you eaten all the sweets?' 'No, there .... (be) still three left.'
5 'What .... (you do) with that chair?' 'Well, the waiter said 'Take a seat'!'
6 'This is your waiter, Paul. He .... (take) your order.'

Creative writing

6) Steve receives an e-mail from an Italian friend:

Hi Steve,

My mum and dad are going to England for their holiday this year – they want me to come with them, because they don't speak English. I said I can't speak English very well, but they don't believe me! They like going out to restaurants, so can you tell me what I should say? Is there anything I need to know about ordering food in your country?

Thanks for your help,

Luigi :-)

Reply to Luigi's e-mail using language you have learnt in this sketch.

....
....
....
....
....
....
....
....
....

The Wise Woman | Worksheet A

Comprehension

1) Listen to the recording then read and circle the correct answer.

1. When the son hears the king's decision, he is:
   a) angry b) frightened c) sad

2. The man hides his mother:
   a) under the floor.
   b) in a secret room.
   c) in the mountains.

3. The king of the east wants:
   a) a drum that talks.
   b) a drum that whistles.
   c) a drum that sounds when nobody beats it.

4. The man's mother suggests:
   a) putting a bee in a drum.
   b) ignoring the king of the east.
   c) playing the drum with a stick.

5. A good title for this play could be:
   a) *The king and the big mountain*
   b) *The old man and the drum*
   c) *The king learns a lesson*

6. The message of the play is that:
   a) we should not listen to old people.
   b) old people are fun.
   c) we must treat old people with respect.

Vocabulary

2) Complete the sentences with a word from the box.

scratch whole mighty scary wise obey

1. When someone tells you what to do, and then you do it, you ………… that person.
2. Something that makes you frightened is ………… .
3. Someone who always has answers to your questions is very ………… .
4. When you don't know the answer to a question, you sometimes ………… your head!
5. If you have a box of chocolates and you eat all of them, you eat the ………… box.
6. ………… is another word for very strong or powerful.

Useful phrases

3) Match 1–6 with a–f.

1. ☐ My English friend says it's raining in Manchester at the moment.
2. ☐ I'm sure I left my phone in your room.
3. ☐ Oh dear, our teacher is going to give us a test tomorrow!
4. ☐ Oh, we'll never get into the school football team.
5. ☐ I don't like swimming underwater.
6. ☐ Here, give your brother this sweet.

a) Oh, that's bad news – I thought it would be an easy day!
b) That's not fair, I haven't got one!
c) I don't think you're right, but you're welcome to look!
d) Believe me, that's not unusual!
e) Well, Mr Sims says he'll give us a chance and let us play in the match tomorrow.
f) It's easy, you just hold your breath.

The Wise Woman | Worksheet B

Grammar 1

4) Complete the sentences with *can, can't, must* or *mustn't*.

1. Is there any way I .... make my computer work faster?
2. You .... bring mobile phones to school now, it's a new rule.
3. I .... play tennis at the moment, I haven't got a racket.
4. I .... save my money because I want a new MP3 player.
5. I .... sleep when there's a lot of noise outside.
6. I .... remember to phone Nikki, she wants to talk to me.

Grammar 2

5) Match 1–6 with a–f.

1. ☐ He doesn't like dogs
2. ☐ This is the shop
3. ☐ The teacher wants to see all the students
4. ☐ That's the girl
5. ☐ It's the team
6. ☐ Don't buy a DVD

a) who are going on the trip to London next week.
b) that only works in America.
c) that sells fashionable clothes.
d) who plays in the regional football team.
e) that bark at everyone.
f) that won the national competition last year.

Creative writing

6) Imagine someone has turned this story into an action film. Write the script for the advert about the film. The advert will be shown in cinemas. Try to make the film sound interesting and exciting. Use phrases like:

- *You've never seen a film like this before!*
- *The old people thought they were safe – they were wrong!*
- *When a king decides, it's time to be afraid!*

Tell parts of the story – you can talk about some of the things the boy does, for example, but don't say what happens at the very end!

....
....
....
....
....
....
....
....

The Reward for Kindness | Worksheet A

Comprehension

1) Read the play then circle (T) True or (F) False.

1. Farmer Smith is counting sheep at the beginning of the play. T / F
2. His wife keeps hitting him because she is angry. T / F
3. The farmer frees the bear because he tells him about a cave in the wood with some treasure in it. T / F
4. All the animals believe the bear is right. T / F
5. At the end of the story, the fox feels disappointed. T / F

Vocabulary

2) Complete the sentences with a word from the box.

| steal | paw | digging | reward | traps | net |

1. What's wrong with your dog? Look, I think his .... is hurting.
2. Mr Cole has lost his wallet. He'll give you a .... if you find it.
3. The best way to catch a lot of fish is with a ....
4. There's a fox in the garden, he's trying to .... our chickens!
5. I don't want these mice in my kitchen. I must buy some ....
6. I'm .... a hole in the garden so I can put this small tree into it.

Grammar

3) Use the prompts and write complete sentences using *going to*.

1. We / go / watch / match / TV this evening
   ....

2. This / how / I go / reward you
   ....

3. I think / they go / win / competition
   ....

4. He says / he / go / trap / fox
   ....

5. You / go / play / this video game / with me?
   ....

6. She / not go / leave school / next year
   ....

The Reward for Kindness | Worksheet B

Useful phrases

4) Match 1–6 with a–f.

1. ☐ I can't keep my eyes open.
2. ☐ I'm really hungry.
3. ☐ He never knows what time it is.
4. ☐ Come on, we're going to be late!
5. ☐ Paul's angry with Barbara, and she's angry with him!
6. ☐ Emma really wants to watch TV.

a) It's time they stopped being so silly!
b) It's time he bought a watch.
c) It's time we started cooking dinner.
d) But it's time she did her homework.
e) It's time I went to bed.
f) It's time we left.

Creative writing

5) Here are adverts for three products. Your friend has a house and is having problems with all these animals. Write an e-mail giving advice about what to do to keep these animals away. Describe the products and how to use them.

ANTI CAT POWDER – cats hate it!

Instructions for use.
1 Watch for where the cat enters your garden.
2 Put *Cat-gone* powder all around the area.
3 Cat will smell the powder and will not come into your garden.

Do not use when raining.

 **Automatic dog barker!**
- Don't let Mr Fox come near your house!
- When a fox comes near the special *Woofo* unit, it automatically starts making a barking sound.
- The fox won't want to stay around for long!

Safetrap – the best mousetrap money can buy.

Don't want mice in your house – but don't want to hurt them?
Use *Safetrap* – simply put some cheese in the trap and leave the door of the trap open.
The mouse enters, the door closes, the mouse can't get out.
Now release the mouse away from your house. Easy!

Rusty Nail Soup | Worksheet A

Comprehension

1) Watch the video of the play then read and circle the correct answer.

1. The woman invites the man in because:
   a) he's tired and hungry.
   b) she likes him.
   c) she isn't afraid.
   d) she thinks he can do something for her.

2. The man:
   a) makes suggestions about what to put in the soup.
   b) tells her about the money she can make.
   c) tells her a story.
   d) tells jokes.

3. The first ingredient the woman puts in the soup is:
   a) salt and pepper.
   b) meat.
   c) a carrot.

4. The woman asks the man his name because:
   a) she is suspicious.
   b) she starts to like him.
   c) she has told him her name.
   d) she is bored.

5. At the end of the play, why isn't the woman angry with the man about the trick he has played?
   a) Because she already knew how to make the soup.
   b) Because she didn't expect the man to tell her about the soup.
   c) Because she enjoyed her evening with the man.
   d) Because she has forgotten everything.

Vocabulary

2) Complete the sentences with the correct word from the box.

| curious   grumpy   suspicious   rusty   delicious   honest |

1. Ross never tells lies.
   He's ………………………………………… .

2. Jenny asks questions all the time – she wants to know everything!
   She's ………………………………………… .

3. Don't talk to Granddad in the morning, he'll never say anything nice until after breakfast.
   He's ………………………………………… .

4. This pudding tastes really good! I love it!
   It's ………………………………………… .

5. I left my bike out in the rain – now look at all the horrible red bits on the metal.
   It's ………………………………………… .

6. I think that person across the road may be a thief.
   I'm ………………………………………… .

Rusty Nail Soup | Worksheet B

Useful phrases

3) Complete the sentences with the letter of the correct phrase.

1 Mmm, these chips are lovely. They could be even better ....
2 I'm bored. I would have plenty to do ....
3 I wish I could talk to Georgia. I could phone her ....
4 I don't know what to cook for lunch. I know, ...
5 I don't know how I'm going to get to the concert. I know, ...
6 My parents said I could do something special for my birthday. Oh, I've an idea – ....

a) I'll ask them if we can go to the beach!
b) I'll use those pizzas I bought yesterday!
c) if only we had some ketchup.
d) I'll ask Karen to take me in her car!
e) if only I had her number.
f) if only I had a laptop.

Grammar

4) Complete the sentences in the first conditional using the correct form of the verbs in brackets.

1 If you put salt in the soup, it .... better. (taste)
2 The horses will come to you if you .... their names. (call)
3 I'll lend you my computer game if you .... to look after it. (promise)
4 We .... to school if it doesn't rain. (walk)
5 I'm sure Conor .... you home if you ask him. (take)
6 If they .... soon, I'm leaving without them. (not come)

Creative writing

5) This play had a happy ending, but imagine the old lady wasn't so happy the next morning and decided to call the police! Write the police report using the answers to the questions below.

- *What time did the man arrive?*
- *What did you think at first?*
- *Why did you let him in?*
- *What did you do all evening?*
- *Why didn't you call the police before you went to bed?*

....
....
....
....
....

The Children and the Wind | Worksheet A

Comprehension

1) Read the play then circle (T) True or (F) False.

1 The children's mother needs some flour to make pancakes.   T / F
2 The wind lives at the top of Mighty Mountain.   T / F
3 The wind gives Hannah the magic chicken first.   T / F
4 The farmer and his wife, Mavis, are good people.   T / F
5 Finally, Billy decides to climb the mountain and talk to the wind.   T / F
6 Billy wants the farmer and Mavis to steal his magic hitting stick.   T / F

Vocabulary

2) Complete the sentences with a word from the box.

cheeky	flour	excited	sensible	naughty	handsome

1 Come on, Billy, stop being so silly! Be .... and help me clean the kitchen.
2 I think Tom Cruise is great! He's so .... !
3 Little Frankie just told his grandma she's fat! Isn't he .... !
4 I need to buy some .... because I want to make pancakes this evening.
5 My little sister's really .... She hid my phone and put salt in dad's tea!
6 We're going to the theme park tomorrow. I can't sleep because I'm so .... !

Dialogue

3) Sammy and his father are having a short holiday at Kay Palmer's Bed and Breakfast. Complete the dialogue with the words and phrases from the box below.

mean to be	Typical
really want you to	at last
Our favourite	Nice meeting you

Father Look, there's Kay's place!
Sammy Oh, ¹....................... ! I thought we'd never arrive!
Father Hi, Kay, lovely to see you.
Kay Hi, Steve. Who's this?
Father This is my son, Sammy.
Kay Hi, Sammy.
²....................... .
Sammy Hi.
Father Hey, Sammy, that was rude!
Sammy Sorry dad, I didn't ³....................... .
Sorry, Mrs Palmer.
Kay Don't worry! Come inside and let me show you your room. I ⁴....................... have a nice stay. Are you hungry? I've made some ham sandwiches.
Father Lovely! ⁵....................... ! Listen Sammy, can you phone mum and tell her we've arrived?
Sammy Oh, I forgot to bring my mobile!
Father ⁶....................... !

The Children and the Wind | Worksheet B

Grammar 1

4) Circle the correct word.

1 Emily wished *for / to* gold and the chicken laid a golden egg.
2 Look, I don't want to talk to you, just go *to / away*!
3 I think that water is very deep. Don't go near it – it's better to keep *out / away*.
4 Oh, here you are! Don't stand outside, come *in / to*!
5 I lent you my video game last week, but can you give it *back / away* to me now, please?
6 Don't come into my room – get *off / out*!

Grammar 2

5) Complete the sentences with the correct form of *be allowed to* or *let*.

1 We .... watch the film last Saturday because we were too young.

2 Nick is going to try to get into the concert without a ticket, but I'm sure they .... him in.

3 **A** Here's a photo of that boy I met on holiday last month.
   B Oh, ... me see!

4 My brother had his seventeenth birthday last week, so now he .... learn to drive.

Creative writing

6) All the neighbours hear about the magic chicken so the local newspaper sends a reporter to ask the children's mother what she will be doing with the money. Read their report below then imagine you win a lot of money in the lottery and write a similar paragraph.

'My daughter wished for gold and the magic chicken laid a golden egg. The first thing I did was buy new clothes for the kids. They really needed some. Then I bought a special little house for the chicken to live in – I want her to be happy! Of course, we all wanted to go on holiday, too. We booked two rooms in a big hotel in Magoc land – you know, the big theme park – and we had a fantastic time! Now we're thinking about buying some fields near here, so our farm will be bigger, but I haven't decided yet. I think we'll need a new egg!'

The Wise Judge | Worksheet

Comprehension

1) Read the play then circle the correct answer.

1. At 5 o'clock:
   a) the woodcutter has to go home.
   b) the judge is coming.
   c) the farmer gets his money.
   d) the woodcutter starts his work.

2. The farmer:
   a) picks up the other axe.
   b) goes back home.
   c) takes the woodcutter's axe.
   d) makes noises.

3. The farmer says he's grunting because:
   a) he's working hard.
   b) he's helping the woodcutter.
   c) he's laughing at the woodcutter.
   d) his back hurts.

4. The woodcutter:
   a) doesn't want to pay the farmer.
   b) wants to pay the farmer.
   c) says the judge will pay him.
   d) isn't working for money.

5. The woodcutter:
   a) wants to wait for the judge.
   b) gives the farmer money.
   c) asks the farmer for money.
   d) phones the judge.

6. The judge:
   a) doesn't arrive.
   b) has no money.
   c) doesn't pay the farmer.
   d) pays both men.

Vocabulary

2) Match 1–6 with a–f.

1. ☐ My watch doesn't work.
2. ☐ You can't keep your eyes open.
3. ☐ This homework is so difficult!
4. ☐ What's the film about?
5. ☐ Hi, Peter, nice to see you!
6. ☐ Here's a pound for Ayesha, and five pounds for you.

a) But that's not fair!
b) Lynn, what a surprise – what brings you here?
c) Maybe I need to buy a new battery.
d) You must be very tired!
e) Can you help me do it?
f) I don't know – let's see what James says, he's seen it.

Grammar

3) Complete the sentences using the present continuous form of the verbs in brackets.

1. What ....? (you do)
2. I .... wood. (cut)
3. My friend .... a house. (build)
4. Ally and Sam .... for the bus. (wait)
5. Pat .... to the teacher. (not listen)
6. Rita and I .... the concert on TV. (watch)

Good Girl | Worksheet A

Comprehension

1) **Read the play then circle (T) True or (F) False.**

   1 The drama teacher wants Ruby to be the servant in the play. T / F
   2 Ruby's parents are too busy at work to come to the play. T / F
   3 Ruby is angry because she is always so kind. T / F
   4 Ruby has dressed as a Goth for a long time. T / F
   5 Ruby's parents like her new look and are not concerned by people's reactions. T / F
   6 At the end of the play, Ruby says she will change her look back to an ordinary one and stop being a Goth. T / F

Vocabulary

2) **Complete the sentences with words from the box.**

   | upset   hectic   by heart   complain   wizard   script |

   1 A man or boy who can do magical things is called a ....
      (Harry Potter is one of these!)
   2 If the food in a restaurant isn't very good, you should ....
   3 If you are an actor in a play or film, you know what to say by reading the
      ....
   4 When you are busy every minute of the day, your life is ....
   5 When someone says something nasty about you, you feel ....
   6 When you learn a poem so you can say it all without reading it, you learn it ....

Useful phrases

3) **Match 1–6 with a–f.**

   1 ☐ Karen's late. I wonder
   2 ☐ This is the painting I did. I think it's good
   3 ☐ I may not be free tomorrow. I'll see you in the morning
   4 ☐ Tommy is horrible to everyone recently! You know,
   5 ☐ I hate this weather. Oh,
   6 ☐ Are you seeing Lily this evening? And

   a) if only it would stop raining!
   b) it's as if he wants to lose all his friends!
   c) if she's missed the bus.
   d) if so, can you tell her to phone me?
   e) though I say so myself.
   f) if possible.

Good Girl | Worksheet B

Grammar

4) Complete the sentences in the 2nd conditional using the correct tense of the verbs in brackets.

1 I'd finish this more quickly if you .... me! (help)
2 The team .... much better if they had a good manager. (play)
3 I would eat this strange thing on my plate if I .... what it was! (know)
4 My dog .... more friendly if you gave him a biscuit. (be)
5 Connie would help you with your work if you .... her. (ask)
6 Laura would only go out with Ted if he .... to take her to a restaurant. (promise)

Useful phrases

5) Match 1–6 with a–f.

1 ☐ If Ruby hadn't dressed as a Goth
2 ☐ Emma wouldn't have got such good results in her exams
3 ☐ We wouldn't have been late
4 ☐ If they had been more careful
5 ☐ You would have known about the party
6 ☐ I would have bought the jeans

a) if you had been ready on time!
b) if you had read my e-mail.
c) the accident would never have happened.
d) nobody would have noticed her.
e) if they had fitted me better.
f) if she hadn't studied for hours every evening.

Creative writing

6) You are the drama teacher at Ruby's school and you want to present a performance of *King Arthur* this July. Design and write the poster for the audition. Things to include:

- *date of performance*
- *the name of the play and what it is about*
- *what the parts are – The Queen, King Arthur, the Wizard, the Good Knight, the Bad Knight, the Bad Knight's mother and the servant*
- *say a little about each part*
- *say how often they will have to come to rehearsals*
- *say when the auditions will take place*

....
....
....
....
....

The Bully | Worksheet A

Comprehension

1) Read the play then circle the correct answer.

1. Jacob tells his mother his trainers are filthy because:
   a) he was caught in the rain.
   b) he was playing football.
   c) he was sitting in mud.
   d) they were in his bag.

2. The story:
   a) tells you what to do if you're bullied.
   b) tells a true story about bullying.
   c) tries to make you laugh.
   d) shows how nasty bullying is.

3. The writer of the play thinks:
   a) everyone should fight against bullies.
   b) that bullies are OK.
   c) bullies aren't a serious problem.
   d) most bullies are basically nice people.

4. Harry hasn't written his essay, but he says it's 'no problem'. Why?
   a) He has written it, in fact.
   b) Someone is going to lend him their essay.
   c) He is going to steal Jacob's essay.
   d) He thinks the teacher won't ask for the essays.

5. The other students:
   a) are against Harry from the beginning.
   b) help Jacob in the end.
   c) are not interested.
   d) help the teacher trap Harry.

6. The teacher asks Harry if he has something to tell him because he:
   a) thinks Harry saw Jacob break the keyboard.
   b) thinks Harry has seen the film.
   c) thinks the film shows what Harry did.
   d) trusts Harry.

Useful phrases

2) Match 1–6 with a–f.

1. ☐ So, are you and Jennie boyfriend and girlfriend now?
2. ☐ Harry, wait, can I talk to you for a moment?
3. ☐ Was Chloe angry when she read the text I sent?
4. ☐ Do you think these trainers are clean enough to wear for the party?
5. ☐ What's that on your face? Have you been fighting?
6. ☐ What do you mean, you think I look fat?!?

a) No, they're filthy!
b) It's not a bruise, it's dirt.
c) That's none of your business!
d) I'd love to have a chat, but I'm in a hurry!
e) Sorry Jessica, it's not true, I was only kidding!
f) She was absolutely furious!

The Bully | Worksheet B

Mini-dialogues

3) Complete the mini-dialogues with phrases from the box.

| leave me alone | What's going on | I'll keep an eye on him |
| Nice try | what a waste of time | |

1 **RUBY** ....? Why are you both smiling like that?

   OLIVIA Oh, nothing … we're just talking!

2 **THOMAS** Hey, Alfie, I went out last night and didn't do my homework. Can I borrow your essay?

   JOSHUA ...., mate, but you know I never lend anyone my work!

3 **SOPHIE** I don't really know what I'm doing – I'll never fix this computer!

   AMELIA Yes, ... Let's leave it and wait for Lily, she's the computer expert.

4 **WILLIAM** Hey, George, what's the matter? You look sad!

   GEORGE Oh, ... I've just had an argument with Emily, and I don't want to talk about it.

5 **CHARLIE** Hey, Jack, can you look after my dog for a minute? I want to go into this shop, and dogs aren't allowed.

   JACK OK, ... Come on boy, let's go for a little walk!

Grammar

4) Circle the correct word to complete the sentences.

1 What's the matter, Zac? Is there *something / everything* you want to tell me?
2 Look, I don't want to talk to you. I haven't got *something / anything* to say.
3 Don't tell Florence about the party, will you? No, I won't say *nothing / anything*.
4 Oh, have you hurt yourself, Dylan? No, it's OK, it's *something / nothing* serious.

Creative writing

5) Write a letter to an advice column about Jacob's problem, asking what he should do. Start like this:

Dear Agony Betty,
My friend Jacob is being bullied at school. Another boy,
....
....
....
....
....

Friendship | Worksheet A

Comprehension

1) Listen to the recording then read and circle the correct answer.

1 Sheri and Lisa have:
   a) never liked each other.
   b) only just got to know each other.
   c) been friends for years and shared a lot.
   d) been friends for a few months.

2 Lisa thinks that if you are a footballer:
   a) you aren't clever.
   b) you're good-looking.
   c) you can only talk about one thing.
   d) Sheri will like you.

3 When Lisa asks if Sheri is coming to the rap show with her:
   a) Sheri thinks about it.
   b) Sheri knows she can't.
   c) Sheri says she will come with her.
   d) Sheri has already decided what she is doing that evening.

4 Sheri argues with Lisa because:
   a) she thinks Lisa will tell Jamie.
   b) she thinks Lisa is on Jenny's side.
   c) she doesn't like the way Lisa talks about Jamie.
   d) she thinks Lisa isn't being honest.

5 Dylan:
   a) is very self-confident.
   b) isn't self-confident.
   c) is too shy to talk to Lisa.
   d) isn't surprised Lisa wants to go out with him.

6 Another title for the play could be:
   a) *An exciting relationship*
   b) *Sheri gets her boy*
   c) *Sheri's bad decision*
   d) *Sheri gets her revenge*

Vocabulary

2) Complete the sentences with words from the box.

| alone   crash   crowd   fool   item   grounded |

1 I saw Zac and Emma kissing at the concert yesterday – I think they're definitely an .... now!

2 Sorry, I can't go to the cinema with you this evening – I got a really bad school report and now I'm ....

3 I really don't like Daniel's new friends – I think he's in with the wrong ....

4 Don't talk to Ruby, she's upset. Just leave her .... for while, she'll be OK.

5 Chloe announced her party on Facebook, so about 200 people tried to .... it on Saturday evening!

6 No, Oliver, don't ask Amelia if you can go out with her – you'll only make a .... of yourself!

Friendship | Worksheet B

Grammar 1

3) Circle the correct word to complete the sentences.

1. My football team lost 6-0 on Saturday. They just didn't put *up / away* a fight.
2. I've always liked Melanie, and yesterday I finally asked her out – I'm looking forward *to / for* this Wednesday!
3. Look, Carl, if you don't go to some of the meetings they're going to kick you *off / out of* the school council.
4. If you want to talk to Anthony, he usually hangs *in / out* with his friends in the music shop.
5. I thought Abbie and Rick had a good relationship, but I heard that Rick is cheating *on / for* her with Nicola.
6. I know that the reason Dawn hasn't got any friends is because she just isn't very nice to people, but I still feel sorry *with / for* her.

Grammar 2

4) Write the sentences using direct speech.

1. You said you were grounded.
   '..,'

2. Josh said he wanted to see Ellie.
   '..,'

3. Tom said he would send Julianne a text the next day.
   '..,'

4. She said she hadn't seen the film.
   '..,'

5. He said he couldn't understand a word you were saying!
   '..,'

Creative writing

5) Write a short paragraph about your best friend. Describe him/her and how long you have known them. Say if you have ever had any problems and, if so, how you resolved them.

....
....
....
....
....
....
....
....

Worksheet Key

1 The Perfect Son

Comprehension 1) 1 d, 2 e, 3 f, 4 a, 5 c, 6 b
Vocabulary 2) excellent, outstanding, superb, awesome, brilliant, wonderful
Grammar 3) 1 get, 2 forgets, 3 tells, 4 use, 5 comes
4) 1 gives, 2 Does … get, 3 plays, 4 takes, 5 watches

2 Smart Shoppers

Comprehension 1) 1 T, 2 F, 3 T, 4 F, 5 T, 6 F, 7 F
Dialogue 2) 1 doesn't go, 2 Let's go, 3 gorgeous, 4 try them, 5 take them, 6 to match
Useful phrases 3) 1 Calm down, 2 let's go, 3 hand me, 4 Hurry up, 5 What's the matter

3 A Fast-Food Stall

Comprehension 1) 1 T, 2 T, 3 F, 4 F, 5 F, 6 T
Mini-Dialogues 2) 1 Here we are, 2 was quick, 3 It doesn't matter, 4 Please hurry, 5 Great service, 6 let's come
Useful phrases 3) 1 d, 2 a, 3 f, 4 c, 5 b, 6 e

4 Colin the Poet

Comprehension 1) 1 T, 2 F, 3 T, 4 F, 5 T, 6 T
Vocabulary 2) 1 (6) marmalade, 2 (3) cheese, 3 (8) butter, 4 (5) orange juice, 5 (2) fried egg, 6 (7) jam, 7 (1) toast, 8 (4) bread
Dialogue 3) 1 Would you like, 2 yes, please, 3 Do you, 4 some, 5 just

5 The Ticket

Comprehension 1) 1 c, 2 d, 3 b, 4 d, 5 d, 6 a
Mini-Dialogues 2) 1 giving, 2 losing, 3 warning, 4 insulting, 5 saying, 6 jumping

6 Being Polite

Comprehension 1) 1 b, 2 a, 3 c, 4 c, 5 b, 6 d
Useful phrases 2) 1 Get me two packets of crisps, right now.
2 Get me a kilo of apples.
3 (example),
4 Good morning. I'd like some cola, please.
5 Would you mind getting me a bar of chocolate?
6 Could you possibly pass the butter, please?

7 Parrot Learns a Lesson

Comprehension 1) 1 c, 2 a, 3 d, 4 a, 5 c, 6 a
Mini-Dialogues 2) 1 to, 2 course, 3 lesson, 4 way, 5 right, 6 into

8 Granddad's Birthday

Comprehension 1) 1 c, 2 a, 3 b, 4 c, 5 d, 6 b
Mini-Dialogues 2) 1 Why don't you, 2 did she like, 3 how did you like, 4 so I took it, 5 so I said, 6 I'm going to

Worksheet Key

9 **The Princess and the Ring**
- Comprehension 1) 1 T, 2 T, 3 F, 4 T, 5 T, 6 F
- Vocabulary 2) 1 bushes, 2 hooligan, 3 swamp, 4 fault, 5 scruffy, 6 drop
- Grammar 3) 1 aren't allowed, 2 can't, 3 can, 4 can't, 5 are allowed, 6 can

10 **At the Doctor's A**
- Comprehension 1) 1 c, 2 b, 3 a, 4 d, 5 a, 6 a
- Useful phrases 2) 1 e, 2 d, 3 b, 4 f, 5 c, 6 a

10 **At the Doctor's B**
- Mini-Dialogues 3) 1 b, 2 c, 3 a, 4 f, 5 d, 6 e
- Grammar 4) 1 rang, 2 was talking, 3 left, 4 was reading, 5 were arguing, 6 were standing
- Useful phrases 5) 1 e, 2 a, 3 f, 4 c, 5 b, 6 d

11 **On Holiday in Rome A**
- Comprehension 1) 1 T, 2 F, 3 T, 4 F, 5 T, 6 F, 7 F, 8 F
- Dialogue 2) 1 a bite to eat, 2 I'm afraid I can't tell you, 3 that's unbelievable, 4 We certainly would, 5 What's it about, 6 So was I

11 **On Holiday in Rome B**
- Dialogue 3) 1 isn't she, 2 can't they, 3 haven't you, 4 could you, 5 will she, 6 isn't she
- Creative writing 4) Students' own answers

12 **At the Hairdresser's A**
- Comprehension 1) 1 f, 2 d, 3 c, 4 b, 5 a, 6 e
- Vocabulary 2) 1 customer, 2 robber, 3 creative, 4 hairdo, 5 bargain, 6 recognises
- Dialogue 3) 1 d, 2 e, 3 a, 4 c, 5 f, 6 b

12 **At the Hairdresser's B**
- Grammar 1 4) 1 met, 2 would have caught, 3 lends, 4 'll/will do, 5 had sent, 6 would like
- Grammar 2 5) 1 's/has been at the restaurant for,
  2 's/has been working as a hairdresser for,
  3 got our dog a long time ago,
  4 has known Connie for ages
- Creative writing 6) Students' own answers

13 **The Space Restaurant A**
- Comprehension 1) 1 b, 2 a, 3 b, 4 b, 5 a, 6 a
- Vocabulary 2) 1 d, 2 a, 3 e, 4 c, 5 b
- Useful phrases 3) 1 e, 2 d, 3 a, 4 f, 5 c, 6 b

Worksheet Key

13		**The Space Restaurant B**
Grammar 1	4)	1 mine, 2 ours, 3 hers, 4 yours, 5 theirs, 6 his
Grammar 2	5)	1 taste, 2 did, 3 will have, 4 are, 5 have you done/did you do, 6 will take
Creative writing	6)	Students' own answers
14		**The Wise Woman A**
Comprehension	1)	1 c, 2 b, 3 c, 4 a, 5 c, 6 c
Vocabulary	2)	1 obey, 2 scary, 3 wise, 4 scratch, 5 whole, 6 mighty
Useful phrases	3)	1 d, 2 c, 3 a, 4 e, 5 f, 6 b
14		**The Wise Woman B**
Grammar 1	4)	1 can, 2 mustn't, 3 can't, 4 must, 5 can't, 6 must
Grammar 2	5)	1 e, 2 c, 3 a, 4 d, 5 f, 6 b
Creative writing	6)	Students' own answers
15		**The Reward for Kindness A**
Comprehension	1)	1 T, 2 F, 3 T, 4 T, 5 T
Vocabulary	2)	1 paw, 2 reward, 3 net, 4 steal, 5 traps, 6 digging
Grammar	3)	1 We're going to watch the match on TV this evening. 2 This is how I'm going to reward you. 3 I think they're going to win the competition. 4 He says he's going to trap the fox. 5 Are you going to play this video game with me? 6 She's not/She isn't going to leave school next year.
15		**The Reward for Kindness B**
Useful phrases	4)	1 e, 2 c, 3 b, 4 f, 5 a, 6 d
Creative writing	5)	Students' own answers
16		**Rusty Nail Soup A**
Comprehension	1)	1 d, 2 a, 3 a, 4 b, 5 c
Vocabulary	2)	1 honest, 2 curious, 3 grumpy, 4 delicious, 5 rusty, 6 suspicious
16		**Rusty Nail Soup B**
Useful phrases	3)	1 c, 2 f, 3 e, 4 b, 5 d, 6 a
Grammar	4)	1 'll/will taste, 2 call, 3 promise, 4 'll/will walk, 5 'll/will take, 6 don't come
Creative writing	5)	Students' own answers
17		**The Children and the Wind A**
Comprehension	1)	1 T, 2 T, 3 F, 4 F, 5 T, 6 F
Vocabulary	2)	1 sensible, 2 handsome, 3 cheeky, 4 flour, 5 naughty, 6 excited
Dialogue	3)	1 at last, 2 Nice meeting you, 3 mean to be, 4 really want you to, 5 Our favourite, 6 Typical

Worksheet Key

17   The Children and the Wind B
- **Grammar 1**   4)   1 for, 2 away, 3 away, 4 in, 5 back, 6 out
- **Grammar 2**   5)   1 weren't allowed to, 2 won't let, 3 let, 4 's/is allowed to
- **Creative writing**   6)   Students' own answers

18   The Wise Judge
- **Comprehension**   1)   1 b, 2 d, 3 b, 4 a, 5 a, 6 c
- **Vocabulary**   2)   1 c, 2 d, 3 e, 4 f, 5 b, 6 a
- **Grammar**   3)   1 are you doing, 2 'm/am cutting, 3 is building, 4 are waiting, 5 isn't listening, 6 are watching

19   Good Girl A
- **Comprehension**   1)   1 T, 2 F, 3 T, 4 F, 5 F, 6 F
- **Vocabulary**   2)   1 wizard, 2 complain, 3 script, 4 hectic, 5 upset, 6 by heart
- **Useful phrases**   3)   1 c, 2 e, 3 f, 4 b, 5 a, 6 d

19   Good Girl B
- **Grammar**   4)   1 helped, 2 would play, 3 knew, 4 would be, 5 asked, 6 promised
- **Useful phrases**   5)   1 d, 2 f, 3 a, 4 c, 5 b, 6 e
- **Creative writing**   6)   Students' own answers

20   The Bully A
- **Comprehension**   1)   1 b, 2 d, 3 a, 4 c, 5 b, 6 c
- **Useful phrases**   2)   1 c, 2 d, 3 f, 4 a, 5 b, 6 e

20   The Bully B
- **Mini-Dialogues**   3)   1 What's going on, 2 Nice try, 3 what a waste of time, 4 leave me alone, 5 I'll keep an eye on him
- **Grammar**   4)   1 something, 2 anything, 3 anything, 4 nothing
- **Creative writing**   5)   Students' own answers

21   Friendship A
- **Comprehension**   1)   1 c, 2 a, 3 d, 4 b, 5 b, 6 c
- **Vocabulary**   2)   1 item, 2 grounded, 3 crowd, 4 alone, 5 crash, 6 fool

21   Friendship B
- **Grammar 1**   3)   1 up, 2 to, 3 off, 4 out, 5 on, 6 for
- **Grammar 2**   4)   1 I'm grounded,
  2 I want to see Ellie,
  3 I'll send Julianne a text tomorrow/I'll send you a text tomorrow, Julianne.
  4 I haven't seen the film,
  5 I can't understand a word you're saying
- **Creative writing**   5)   Students' own answers

Quick-reference guide

This guide will help you select a play suitable for your class based on its approximate runtime, the learning level(s) of your students, the number of roles and the language focus.

To use the guide, look down the 'Performance time' column till you come to a runtime that matches your requirements, and then look across to see the name of the activity under the level it's suited to. Then across again to find the number of roles, the language focus and the play number.

If you prefer to start with the level of your students, find that on the top line, then go down till you find an activity name; on that row you will find the runtime, the number of roles, the language focus and the play number.

Elementary A2	Intermediate B1	Upper Intermediate B2	Language focus	Number of roles	Performance time (mins)	DVD	Audio CD	Play page number	Worksheet page number	Play number
Chapter 1: Short sketches										
The Perfect Son			Present simple, third person singular, verb phrases	2–5	2		✓	p.36	p.185	1
Smart Shoppers			Language for clothes shopping; making suggestions; telling someone what to do	3	2		✓	p.40	p.186	2
A Fast-Food Stall			Ordering food; polite requests, and how they change when in a hurry	7	5		✓	p.43	p.187	3
Colin the Poet			Politely accepting and refusing offers; breakfast; rhyming pairs	6	5		✓	p.48	p.188	4
	The Ticket		Gerunds; conditional 2; apologising	3	3		✓	p.53	p.189	5
	Being Polite		Going shopping; degrees of politeness/rudeness	6	6	✓		p.56	p.190	6
	Parrot Learns a Lesson		Giving advice; imperatives (affirmative and negative)	5–8	5		✓	p.62	p.191	7
	Granddad's Birthday		Giving advice; expressing intentions; asking if someone liked a present; narrating	4–8	5		✓	p.66	p.192	8
		The Princess and the Ring	Can/can't; be allowed to; making and refusing offers	5	5		✓	p.71	p.193	9
		At the Doctor's	Medical expressions; past tenses	11	10			p.77	p.194	10
Chapter 2: Medium-length sketches										
	On Holiday in Rome		High-frequency chunks; tag questions	9–14	10		✓	p.88	p.196	11
	At the Hairdresser's		Idioms; deciding what to do; *if*-clauses; *will*-future; present perfect	4–6	12			p.96	p.198	12
	The Space Restaurant		Possessive pronouns; ordering food and drink	Approx 13	10	✓		p.106	p.200	13
Chapter 3: Medium-length plays based on traditional stories										
	The Wise Woman		Formal language; *must, can't, unless*; defining relative clauses	14	8		✓	p.116	p.202	14
	The Reward for Kindness		Expressing intention; *it's time* + past tense	7	5			p.122	p.204	15
	Rusty Nail Soup		*if only*; *will*-future	10	4	✓		p.127	p.206	16
	The Children and the Wind		Making requests; exclamations	8	20			p.133	p.208	17
The Wise Judge			Present continuous	3	4			p.148	p.210	18
Chapter 4: Teenage dramas										
	Good Girl		*Will*-future; *going to*-future	7–14	14			p.154	p.211	19
	The Bully		Something/anything/nothing/everything; chunks of language	Min 10	7			p.165	p.213	20
	Friendship		Expressions about people and relationships	5–10+	14	✓	✓	p.172	p.215	21

DVD Contents and Audio CD Tracklist

 **DVD CONTENTS**

Sample plays

- Being Polite
- The Space Restaurant
- Rusty Nail Soup
- The concept of a 'split scene'

Tips and guidelines for staging and performing a play

Introduction

Voice projection
- Backs are bad/Upstaging
- Seeing is hearing
- Throw your voice
- A column of sound
- Not the Opera House!

Staging and 'blocking'
- Blocking
- What did I do last time?
- NOT straight lines
- Back foot, front foot
- Sight lines

Concentration and focus
- Don't fiddle!
- Mirroring/Be 'in the moment'
- If it itches, scratch it!
- Enjoy it, relax ... nothing can go wrong!
- Staying in character: acting is also reacting

Building the characters to tell your story
- Gesture
- How does my character stand and walk? Who does my character remind me of?
- Hands
- There's no such thing as a small part

Pace
- Picking up cues
- Don't let your character pick up another character's pace
- Don't rush through the 'boring bits'
- Emphasis and repetition
- Knowing when to stop

Remembering or learning lines

And finally ...

 AUDIO CD TRACKLIST
Track 00

01 The Perfect Son	01:51	Music for *Friendship*:
02 Smart Shoppers	02:03	12 Music for Prelude and
03 A Fast-Food Stall	02:46	into Scene 1 and 6 *Friendship* 01:03
04 Colin the Poet	02:17	13 Music for Scene 2 *Party* 01:48
05 The Ticket	01:42	14 Music for Scene 4 and 5 *Pill* 02:27
06 Parrot Learns a Lesson	03:18	15 Music for Scene 7 *1, 2, 3, 4* 00:41
07 Granddad's Birthday	04:08	16 Music for Scene 7 *Bad Party* 02:56
08 The Princess and the Ring	07:12	**TOT 61:23**
09 On Holiday in Rome	08:25	
10 The Wise Woman	07:25	
11 Friendship	10:37	